NEXT MOVE

STUDENTS' BOOK

FIONA BEDDALL AND JAYNE WILDMAN

3

Contents

Reading and Listening	Speaking and Pronunciation	Writing
School Intranet	Asking for and giving personal information	A personal profile
Live Small What does your bedroom say about you ◉ Hannah's bedroom ◉ Dictation	Describing a place **Pronunciation:** /v/, /w/ and /b/	A description of a room **Writing File:** Linking words: addition and contrast
Click! Magazine: young photographer competition Great moments in history ◉ Talking about a photo ◉ Dictation	Permission **Pronunciation:** Sentence stress	A description of a picture **Writing File:** Describing a picture
London market wins award The internet – the world's biggest market ◉ Problems with buying things online ◉ Dictation	Asking for help **Pronunciation:** /ɒ/ and /əʊ/	A customer review **Writing File:** Expressing opinion
Survey: Teens and the media Profile: Christiane Amanpour ◉ Opinions about the news ◉ Dictation	Doubt and disbelief **Pronunciation:** /æ/ and /aː/	A profile **Writing File:** Error correction
Behind the camera Strange tourist attractions ◉ Radio interview ◉ Dictation	Asking for information **Pronunciation:** /aɪ/ vs /ɪ/	A travel guide **Writing File:** Making your writing more interesting
Today's teens don't do chores Future teens ◉ Teenagers of the future ◉ Dictation	Giving advice **Pronunciation:** /ʌ/ and /juː/	A problem page **Writing File:** Linking words: reason and result
London Elephant Parade Do something different … ◉ An interview about a charity ◉ Dictation	Persuading **Pronunciation:** *going to*	A formal letter **Writing File:** Letter writing
Interview: Naomi Daniels Why are people risk-takers? ◉ Talking about a TV show ◉ Dictation	Talking about health **Pronunciation:** *gh*	An application form **Writing File:** Completing an application form
Teenage inventors A book for all time? ◉ Reading stories on a smartphone ◉ Dictation	Problems with machines **Pronunciation:** /ɪ/ and /iː/	An opinion essay **Writing File:** How to write an opinion essay

■ **Curriculum File**   ■ **Real World Profiles**

Starter Unit

Grammar and Vocabulary

to be

1 Complete the sentences with the correct form of *to be*.

  1 My brother *is* only ten so he .... (not) at my school.
  2 They .... (not) at home. Where .... (they)?
  3 ' .... (we) late for school?' 'Yes, you .... .'
  4 I .... (not) British. I .... American.
  5 ' .... there a shopping centre in town?' 'Yes, there .... , but there .... (not) any good shops in it.'

have got

2 Choose the correct options.

  1 I *have / has* got a new pen.
  2 *Has she got / She has got* any brothers or sisters?
  3 *He've / He's* got some difficult homework tonight.
  4 The film *haven't / hasn't* got any good actors in it.
  5 Have *got you / you got* time for a coffee?
  6 We *haven't / haven't got* a dog.

be and have got

3 Look at the picture and complete the sentences. Use the correct form of *be* or *have got*, positive or negative.

  1 He *hasn't got* fair hair.
  2 She .... beautiful.
  3 They .... curly hair.
  4 He .... well-built.
  5 He .... long hair.
  6 She .... brown eyes.
  7 He .... handsome.
  8 She .... slim.

Possessive 's

4 Complete the sentences with *'s* or *s'*.

  1 She's *William's* (William) sister.
  2 Those are my .... (friend) shoes.
  3 The .... (dogs) legs are very short.
  4 I can't see over the .... (people) heads.
  5 The .... (man) hat is on the chair.
  6 Look at those .... (girls) hair styles!

is, has and possessive 's

5 Look at the *'s* in these sentences. Is it *is, has* or possessive?

  1 The student**'s** name is Hannah. *possessive*
  2 He**'s** in London.
  3 Katie**'s** got a computer.
  4 It**'s** a sunny day.
  5 The book**'s** under the bed.
  6 The book**'s** pages are dirty.
  7 She**'s** got a big family.
  8 Dan**'s** mum has got a new job.

Subject and object pronouns

6 Choose the correct words.

  1 She likes Matt but *she / her* doesn't like James.
  2 You can visit *they / them* tomorrow.
  3 Please listen to *I / me*.
  4 *He / Him* has got a new car.
  5 My grandparents don't live with *we / us*.
  6 I want to help *she / her*.
  7 Why do *they / them* like golf? It's boring!
  8 When my brother plays football, we watch *he / him*.

Possessive adjectives

7 Rewrite the sentences. Use possessive adjectives.

  1 I've got a very old computer.
    My computer is very old.

  2 It has got a small screen.
  3 You've got nice parents.
  4 They've got red hair.
  5 He's got a new T-shirt.
  6 We've got difficult homework.
  7 She's got a very clever brother.

Common verbs

8 Match the verbs (1–8) to the activities in the picture (a–h).

1 fly *b*   5 sail
2 eat   6 climb
3 play   7 jump
4 run   8 swim

Prepositions

9 Look at the picture in Exercise 8. Complete the sentences with these words.

around	behind	in front of	into	next to
~~on~~	over	under	up	

1 There's a tower *on* the island.
2 A man is sailing .... the island.
3 A plane is flying .... the beach.
4 The sun is .... a cloud.
5 A girl is sitting .... the tent.
6 There's a CD player .... the girl.
7 A boy is climbing .... a tree.
8 His friend is jumping .... the sea.
9 A ball is .... a chair.

Indefinite pronouns

10 Complete the conversation with these words.

anything	~~everyone~~	everything	no one
someone	something		

A Where is ¹ *everyone* today?
B They're all at the beach.
A Oh yes! ² .... invited me, too. Who was it? Kate, I think.
B You're lucky. ³ .... invited me.
A Oh, I'm sorry.
B I don't mind. I don't like swimming and I haven't got ⁴ .... to wear at the beach.
B Come and buy ⁵ .... new at the shops now! What about a new T-shirt?
A No. ⁶ .... in the shops at the moment is expensive and I haven't got any money.

Everyday objects

11 Match the beginnings of the words to the endings. Then match the words to the pictures.

1 maga — book
2 cam — et
3 lap — per
4 wall — ns
5 note — zine *picture e*
6 pos — top
7 wa — era
8 jum — ter
9 jea — tch

School subjects

12 Complete the words (1–8). Then match them to the pictures (a–h).

1 S c i e n c e   *picture c*
2 M a _ _ s
3 H _ _ _ _ r y
4 G e o g _ _ _ _ _
5 E _ _ l i _ _
6 M u s _ _
7 A _ _
8 L _ t _ _ _ t _ _ _

Present simple: affirmative and negative

13 Complete the sentences with the correct form of the verbs.

1 She *doesn't live* (not live) here.
2 They .... (not eat) vegetables.
3 He .... (fly) to the USA every summer.
4 She .... (watch) TV in the evenings.
5 We .... (get up) at seven o'clock.
6 It .... (not work).
7 You .... (not know) Liam.
8 I .... (have) a shower every day.

Present simple: questions and short answers

14 Complete the questions and then answer them.

1 *Do you like* (you/like) Science? ☑ *Yes, I do.*
2 .... (Jessica/learn) English? ☒
3 .... (we/do) PE on Tuesdays? ☒
4 .... (they/study) Maths at the weekends? ☑
5 .... (I/need) a new Geography book? ☒
6 .... (he/teach) History? ☑

Adverbs of frequency

15 Write these words in the sequence.

always	hardly ever	~~never~~
often	sometimes	usually

0%
1 *never*
2 ....
3 ....
4 ....
5 ....
100%
6 ....

16 Make true sentences. Use adverbs of frequency.

1 I / late / for school

I am sometimes late for school.

2 My class / listen / to the teacher
3 We / do / our homework
4 Our lessons / interesting
5 I / take / the bus / to school
6 My friends / walk / home from school / with me

Numbers and dates

17 What are the missing numbers and words?

1 13   *thirteen*
2 ....   seven hundred and twenty-two
3 490   ....
4 ....   six thousand, one hundred and ten
5 3,412   ....
6 ....   eight million
7 16,091   ....
8 ....   thirty thousand, five hundred

18 How do we say these dates?

1 1 Jan *January the first*   5 8 Nov
2 3 Aug   6 25 Apr
3 14 Mar   7 23 Dec
4 2 Sept   8 31 Oct

was/were

19 Complete the conversation with the correct form of *was/were*.

A When were you born?
B I ¹ *was* born on 2ⁿᵈ July 1997. And I ² .... (not) born in this country. My parents ³ .... in Kenya.
A Why ⁴ .... they there?
B My mum ⁵ .... a nurse there and my dad ⁶ .... an engineer.
A ⁷ .... they happy in Kenya?
B Yes, they ⁸ .... , but there ⁹ .... (not) any good schools near our home in Kenya. That's why we live here now.

Opinion adjectives

20 Complete the adjectives in these sentences.

1 A lot of classical music is very r o m a n t i c.
2 Science fiction films are very e x _ _ t _ _ g.
3 Mexican food is very t _ s _ y.
4 A lot of animated films are very f _ _ n _ .
5 Rap music is r _ b _ _ s h.
6 This is a b r _ l l _ _ n t football match!
7 Museums are b _ r _ _ g.
8 Pony trekking is e _ p _ _ s _ v _ .
9 Rock climbing is s c _ r _ .
10 A tarantula is a w _ _ r d pet!
11 A lot of children's TV shows are _ n _ o y _ _ g.

21 Give your opinion. Make six sentences, using adjectives from Exercise 20 and some of these words.

action films	documentaries	horror films	musicals
fish	pasta	vegetables	
jazz	opera	rock music	
bowling	judo	skateboarding	surfing

Skateboarding is an exciting sport.

Speaking and Listening

1 🔊 1.2 **Read and listen to the conversation. Correct the answers.**

Ruby
1 Where are you from?
   I'm from ~~the UK~~. *New Zealand*
2 Why do you live in the UK now?
   Because my dad has got a new job here.
3 When did you move to the UK?
   Yesterday.
4 How old are you?
   I'm seventeen.

Tom
5 Who have you got in your family?
   My mum, my dad and my sister, Ruby.
6 Which road does your family live on?
   Ash Road.
7 How do you go to school?
   I go by bike.
8 When do you leave in the morning?
   Eight o'clock.

2 **Act out the conversation in groups of four.**

Ruby Excuse me, where's room 27?
Ella It's on the left here. We can show you.
Ruby Thanks.
Ash Are you new at this school?
Ruby Yes. I only moved to this country last week.
Ash Welcome to the UK! Where are you from?
Ruby New Zealand, but my mum has got a job here now.
Tom Where do you live?
Ruby On Talbot Road.
Ella We live there, too – at number 72. What about you?
Ruby Our house is number 73!
Tom Cool! We can see your house from our window. I'm Tom. This is my sister, Ella, and this is our friend, Ash. We're all fourteen.
Ruby Me, too! Hi, guys. I'm Ruby.
Ella Hey, do you want to walk to school with us tomorrow? We usually leave at quarter past eight.
Ruby Sure! Thanks.

3 **Complete the sentences from the conversation.**
1 *Welcome* to the UK!
2 What .... you?
3 I'm Tom. .... is my sister, Ella.
4 Hi, ... I'm Ruby.

8

Reading

4 Read the page from the school website.

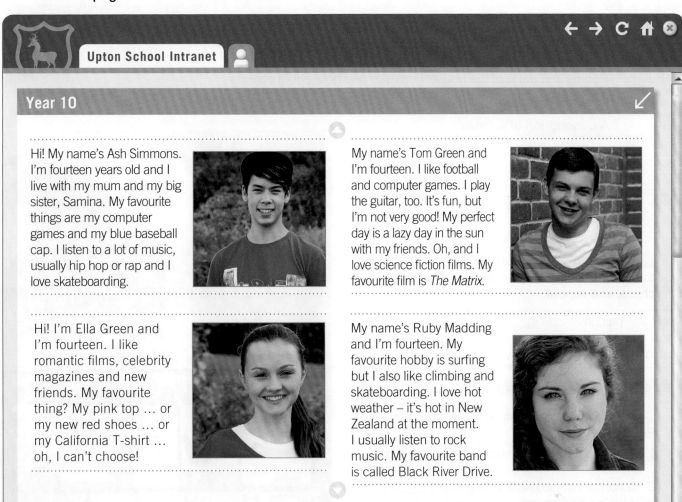

Upton School Intranet

Year 10

Hi! My name's Ash Simmons. I'm fourteen years old and I live with my mum and my big sister, Samina. My favourite things are my computer games and my blue baseball cap. I listen to a lot of music, usually hip hop or rap and I love skateboarding.

My name's Tom Green and I'm fourteen. I like football and computer games. I play the guitar, too. It's fun, but I'm not very good! My perfect day is a lazy day in the sun with my friends. Oh, and I love science fiction films. My favourite film is *The Matrix*.

Hi! I'm Ella Green and I'm fourteen. I like romantic films, celebrity magazines and new friends. My favourite thing? My pink top … or my new red shoes … or my California T-shirt … oh, I can't choose!

My name's Ruby Madding and I'm fourteen. My favourite hobby is surfing but I also like climbing and skateboarding. I love hot weather – it's hot in New Zealand at the moment. I usually listen to rock music. My favourite band is called Black River Drive.

5 Read the website again. Copy and complete the table.

Name	Ash …
Likes	computer games, …. , …. and rap music, ….
Name	…. Green
Likes	…. films, …. magazines, new …. , clothes
Name	Tom ….
Likes	…. , computer games, the …. , …. films
Name	Ruby Madding
Likes	…. , climbing, …. , …. weather, …. music

Writing

6 Make your profile for the school website.

New Member

My name's …. .
I'm …. years old.
I live with …. .
I like/love …. .
My favourite …. is/are …. .

✓ **My assessment profile:** Workbook page 126

1 Home Sweet Home

Grammar	Present simple and continuous; Verb + -ing
Vocabulary	Rooms and parts of the house; Furniture and household objects
Speaking	Describing a place
Writing	A description of a room

Vocabulary Rooms and parts of the house

1 🔊 1.3 **Match the pictures of the parts of the house (1–16) to these words. Then listen, check and repeat.**

attic	balcony	ceiling	cellar	drive	fireplace
floor	garage	hall	landing	lawn	office
patio 1	roof	stairs	wall		

Word list page 43   **Workbook** page 104

2 **Complete the sentences with the words in Exercise 1.**

1 The *stairs* go up to the bedrooms at the top of a house.
2 You come into the house through the _ _ _ _ .
3 There's a bird on the _ _ _ _ .
4 The _ _ _ _ _ _ is next to the bathroom.
5 The red car is inside the _ _ _ _ _ _ .
6 There are boxes of old toys in the _ _ _ _ _ .
7 It's warm near the _ _ _ _ _ _ _ _ _ in the living room.
8 Someone is cutting the grass on the _ _ _ _ .

3 **Tell a partner about your home.**

1 Have you got a house or a flat?
2 Describe the outside of your house or flat.
   • Is it big or small?
   • What colour are the walls and roof?
   • Is there a balcony, a lawn, a garage, a drive?
3 Describe the inside of your house or flat.
   • Is there a hall, an attic, a cellar, an office?
   • What colour are the walls, floor and ceiling in your bedroom and your living room?

> *Our house is small. It's got white walls and a red roof. There's a garden with a small patio and a lawn. There's a drive, but there isn't a garage.*

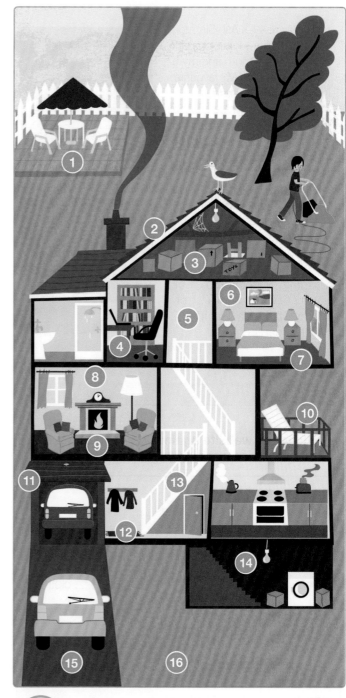

Brain Trainer Unit 1
Activity 2 Go to page 112

Reading

1 Look at the photo. What do you think this building is for?

2 Read the text quickly. Choose the best answer.

  1 Austin is a *schoolboy / builder*.
  2 The building is *his bedroom / a complete house*.
  3 He wants to *live in it / sell it*.

3 🔊 1.4   Read the text again. Answer the questions.

  1 How are families in Europe and North America changing?
    The size of an average family is getting smaller.
  2 What are the disadvantages of big homes?
  3 Where is Austin's bedroom?
  4 What is 3.7 metres long?
  5 What does Austin like about his house?
  6 What happens when a building job is difficult for Austin?
  7 Does Austin live in his house all the time? Why?/Why not?
  8 Why is his house useful for the future?

4 In pairs, ask and answer.

  1 Are many homes in your country bigger than they need to be?
  2 Imagine your family in a house that is half the size of your home now. How is your life different? What is better? What is worse?
  3 Would you like to live on your own in a house like Austin's? Why?/Why not?

© Tumbleweed Tiny House company

Live Small

In Europe and North America, the size of an average family is getting smaller, but homes are not. In many countries they are getting bigger. Bigger homes are more expensive and heating them in cold weather is worse for the environment. Many people believe it's time to think again about the size of our homes. Sixteen-year-old Austin Hay is building a home on his parents' drive. It's got everything important, including a shower room, a kitchen and an attic bedroom with a low ceiling, but it's only 2.4 metres wide and 3.7 metres long.

'When I was a kid, I wanted to build a tree house,' Austin explains. 'But this house is on wheels and that's a lot cooler.'

Austin doesn't do any building during the week – he's busy with school work and playing baseball. But he usually works hard on his house at the weekend. 'At the moment I'm working on the doors. They're quite easy, so my dad isn't helping me. He only helps with the difficult things.'

Austin is sleeping in his little house this summer. There isn't a fireplace at the moment, so in winter he'll move back across the lawn to his parents' house. And in the future? 'University is very expensive in the USA, but it'll be cheaper for me because I can take my little house with me. I can live in it anywhere.'

Grammar Present simple and continuous

Present simple	Present continuous
He always makes nice food.	He is making dinner at the moment.
I live with my dad.	They're staying in a house without any adults.

> Grammar reference Workbook page 86

1 Study the grammar table. Match the sentence beginnings (1–2) to the endings (a–d) to complete the rules.

> **1** We use the Present simple
> **2** We use the Present continuous
>
> > **a** for routines and habits.
> > **b** for actions in progress.
> > **c** for temporary situations.
> > **d** for permanent situations and general truths.

2 Choose the correct options.

1 Sophie and Kat *don't talk / aren't talking* to me today.
2 I *always go / am always going* to bed at nine o'clock.
3 We *often go / are often going* to the cinema at the weekend.
4 *I'm learning / I learn* about electricity in Science this week.
5 British people *use / are using* a lot of electricity in their homes.
6 Where's Kieran? *Does he have / Is he having* a shower?

3 Complete the phone conversation with the Present continuous form of the verbs.

A Hi, Ellie. How are you?
B Fine thanks, Gran.
A How ¹ *are you feeling* (you/feel) about your exams?
B Not too bad, thanks. I ² .... (study) on the balcony at the moment.
A ³ .... (the sun/shine) there?
B Yes, it ⁴ .... (shine). It's lovely!
A You're lucky! Your grandad and I ⁵ .... (wear) our coats in the house because it's so cold! What ⁶ .... (Callum and Leo/do)?
B They ⁷ .... (listen) to music in the cellar. Do you want to talk to them?
A Actually, I want to talk to your dad.
B OK. He ⁸ .... (wash) the car on the drive. Wait a minute …

4 Complete the text with the Present simple or Present continuous form of the verbs.

I usually ¹ *have* (have) a bath before bed but tonight I ² .... (wait) on the landing. Why? Because my brothers Mick and Todd ³ .... (use) the bathroom for band practice. Most people ⁴ .... (not wear) their clothes in the bath, but Todd is different. At the moment he ⁵ .... (lie) in the bath with all his clothes on. Mick ⁶ .... (sit) on the side of the bath and he ⁷ .... (play) something on the guitar. They usually ⁸ .... (practise) their band music in the garage, but my mum ⁹ .... (paint) flowers on her car in there tonight! I ¹⁰ .... (live) with the world's craziest family!

5 Make questions.

1 you / always / have / a shower or bath / before bed?
Do you always have a shower or bath before bed?
2 what time / you / usually / go to bed?
3 you / often / get up / late / at the weekend?
4 you / listen / to music / at the moment?
5 where / you / usually / do / your homework?
6 you / work / hard / right now?

6 **What about you?** In pairs, ask and answer the questions in Exercise 5.

> *Do you always have a shower or bath before bed?*

> *No, I usually have a shower in the morning.*

Vocabulary Furniture and household objects

1 🔊 1.5 **Match the pictures (1–13) to these words. Then listen, check and repeat.**

alarm clock	armchair	blind	bookcase
chest of drawers	curtains	cushions	duvet
mirror	pillow	rug	vase
wardrobe 1			

Word list page 43   **Workbook** page 104

2 **Read the descriptions. Say the thing or things.**

1 You put clothes in this. (two things)
   a wardrobe and a chest of drawers
2 You can see your face in this.
3 You put flowers in this.
4 This wakes you up in the morning.
5 You put books in this.
6 This is on the floor. You can walk on it.
7 When you are using these, you can't see out of the window. (two things)
8 You sit in this.
9 This keeps you warm in bed.
10 You put your head on this in bed.
11 You put these on your bed or on a chair.

3 **Which things from Exercise 1 are in your home? Make sentences.**

There's a bookcase in the hall, next to the living room door.

Pronunciation /v/, /w/ and /b/

4a 🔊 1.6 **Listen and repeat.**

balcony	bookcase	drive
vase	wall	window

b 🔊 1.7 **Listen and repeat. Then practise saying the sentences.**

1 My favourite vase in the living room is very heavy.
2 Why did you wash the windows and walls?
3 There's a big blue blind above the bookcase.
4 I love black and white duvets.
5 Do you want to have a shower before breakfast?

5 **Say a sentence about the picture in Exercise 1. Your partner says *True* or *False*.**

There's a blue rug on the floor.

False! There's a green rug on the floor.

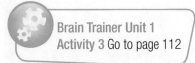

Brain Trainer Unit 1
Activity 3 Go to page 112

Chatroom Describing a place

Speaking and Listening

1 Look at the photo. Whose house do you think this is?

2 🔊 1.8 Listen and read the conversation. Check your answer.

3 🔊 1.8 Listen and read again. Choose the correct options.

1 Ruby *wants / doesn't want* to move house again soon.
2 Ash *likes / doesn't like* Ruby's new house.
3 Ruby's bedroom is *big / small*.
4 There's a computer in *Ruby's bedroom / the office*.
5 Ash *wants / doesn't want* to go into the living room.
6 Ella *likes / doesn't like* the town.

4 Act out the conversation in groups of four.

Ruby	Thanks for carrying these boxes in from the drive, guys.
Tom	No problem! We don't mind helping.
Ruby	I can't stand moving house. I never want to see another cardboard box again!
Ash	Your new house is really cool.
Ruby	Thanks, Ash.
Ella	What's your bedroom like?
Ruby	It's a bit small, but that's OK. There's space for a chest of drawers and a little desk for my computer. Anyway, I prefer spending time in the garden.
Ella	What's behind that door?
Ruby	The living room. It's got a big door out to the patio.
Ash	Let's go out there now. It's a lovely day.
Tom	Hang on! Let's show Ruby the town first.
Ruby	I'd like that. What's the town like?
Ella	It isn't very big, but it's quite nice.
Ash	Come on, then. Let's go!

Say it in your language …

guys
No problem!
I'd like that.
Come on, then.

5 **Look back at the conversation. Find these expressions.**

1 a question asking about Ruby's bedroom

What's your bedroom like? (Ella)

2 an expression describing Ruby's bedroom

3 a question asking about the town

4 two expressions describing the town

6 **Read the phrases for describing a place.**

Describing a place		
What's it like?		
It's	**a bit** **quite** **very** **really**	small.

7 🔊 **1.9** **Listen to the conversations. Act out the conversations in pairs.**

Ruby What's ¹ your bedroom like?

Ella It's got ² pretty red walls and a white wardrobe.

Ruby Is it ³ quite big?

Ella Yes, it is.

Ruby What's ⁴ the swimming pool like?

Ash It's very nice. It's ⁵ quite cold but it's got ⁶ a lovely café.

8 **Work in pairs. Replace the words in purple in Exercise 7. Use these words and/or your own ideas. Act out the conversations.**

What's your garden like?

It's got a lawn and lots of flowers.

1	your kitchen / your living room / your bathroom

2	green walls and a cooker / white walls and a big sofa / pink walls and a large bath

3	a bit small / very big / really small

4	the park / the library / the shopping centre

5	quite small / very quiet / really busy

6	a lake / lots of interesting books / some boring shops

Grammar Verb + -ing

I prefer spending time in the garden.

Tom, Ash and Ella don't mind helping Ruby.

Ruby can't stand moving house.

Do you like living here?

> **Grammar reference** Workbook page 86

1 **Study the grammar table. Complete the rule.**

> After the verbs *like, love, hate, enjoy, don't mind,* .... and .... , we use verb + *-ing*.

2 **Complete the sentences with the correct form of these verbs.**

do	get	listen	~~live~~	sleep	swim	wait

1 He doesn't like *living* in England because it's colder than Spain.

2 She hates beds. She prefers .... on the floor.

3 I can't stand .... to rap music.

4 They love .... in the sea.

5 We don't mind .... our homework.

6 Do you prefer .... up late in the morning?

7 I don't enjoy .... for buses in the rain.

3 **Complete the second sentence so it has a similar meaning to the first sentence. Use the correct form of the word in brackets and one other word.**

1 I think skateboarding is OK. (mind)

I *don't mind* skateboarding.

2 She never wants to have breakfast. (not like)

She .... having breakfast.

3 He's very happy when he rides his bike. (love)

He .... his bike.

4 It's better when we have band practice in the cellar. (prefer)

We .... band practice in the cellar.

5 They hate doing homework. (not stand)

They .... doing homework.

4 **Make three questions with *Do you like + -ing*. Then ask and answer in pairs.**

Do you like going to the beach?

Yes, I love it. What about you?

I don't mind it, but I prefer going to a swimming pool.

Reading

1 Read the magazine article quickly. Choose the best heading.
1 Tidy your room!
2 What does your bedroom say about you?
3 How to have a cool bedroom

You can't always choose your room, but you can choose the things inside it. Because of that, your bedroom says a lot about your personality.

And we're not only talking about your favourite hobbies or your taste in music and books. Of course, a guitar behind the door or sci-fi stories in your bookcase give people information about you, but a careful look at your bedroom can teach them a lot more than that.

The colours in your room, for example, are very interesting. Has your room got bright colours on the walls, curtains, rug or duvet? Then you probably love trying new experiences. People with pale walls are often friendly and talkative, but people with dark walls don't like meeting new people. Black and white is a popular choice for people with strong opinions.

How big is your wardrobe? A big wardrobe often means that you are into fashion, but not always. It can also be a sign that you hate throwing old things away and prefer keeping everything behind your wardrobe door. Someone with a tidy room is usually cheerful, but someone with an untidy room is moodier and often unhappy. The pictures on your walls say a lot, too. Generous people like decorating their rooms with photos of their friends and family, but if your own face is in every picture or you have more than one mirror, watch out! This shows that you are probably a bit selfish.

So, before you invite your friends into your bedroom, think carefully. What message will your bedroom give them about you?

Key Words

| taste | careful | bright |
| pale | be into | decorate |

2 🔊 1.10 Read the article again. Answer the questions.

1 What two things give information about your tastes and interests?
The colours in your room and the pictures on the walls.

2 What type of colours do shy people often have on their walls?

3 Why do people have big wardrobes? Find two reasons in the article.

4 You are usually smiling. What does the article say about your room?

5 You like buying presents for people. What do you probably have on your walls?

6 What two things show that a person thinks only about him/herself?

Listening

1 🔊 1.11 Hannah is talking to a friend about her bedroom and the article above. Listen and choose the correct options.

1 How much of the article is correct about her?
a all of it **b** a lot of it **c** some of it **d** nothing

2 Does she want:
a a tidier room? **b** a lock on her door?

🔊 Listening Bank Unit 1 page 118

2 In pairs, ask and answer. Is the article right about you?
1 What colour are your bedroom walls?
2 Have you got any bright colours in your bedroom?
3 Are there any pictures of your friends on the walls?
4 Are there any pictures of you?
5 How many mirrors are there?
6 Is your room tidy?

Writing   A description of a room

1   Read the Writing File.

Writing File   Linking words:
addition and contrast

You can link similar ideas with *and, also* and *too*.
You're really talkative and you like having new experiences.
The rug is green. The duvet is *also* green.
The colours are interesting. The pictures are interesting, *too*.

You can link contrasting ideas with *but* and *however*.
I've got some pictures of friends, but I haven't got any pictures of myself.
I love red. However, I don't like the bright red walls in my living room.

2   Read about Matt's favourite room. Find the linking words.

My favourite room
by Matt Davies

My favourite room is the office at home. It's a bit small, but it's really light and it's always very quiet. There's a big desk under the window. On the desk there's a computer and a lamp. There's a box of pens and pencils, too. In front of the desk there's a chair with green cushions and next to it there's a bookcase full of interesting books. The walls are white and there's a blue and green blind on the window. The rug in front of the desk is also blue and green.
I love sitting at the desk and watching all the people in the street. I usually do my homework in the room. However, when I don't have any homework, I like playing games on the computer.

3   Complete the sentences with *and, also, too, but* and *however*.

1 He's got a big wardrobe for his clothes *and* he's got two big chests of drawers.
2 My alarm clock wakes me up in the morning and it can play the radio, ...
3 We watch TV in the kitchen and we .... do our homework there.
4 I like playing tennis. ...., I don't play very often.
5 I've got three pet lizards in my bedroom and I've .... got a pet snake.
6 There's a pillow on the bed, ... there isn't a duvet.
7 Her pink armchair is very pretty. ...., she never sits on it.
8 I live with my mum, and my grandparents live with us, ...

4   Read Matt's description again. Answer the questions.

1 What room is it? *The office.*
2 What adjectives does he use to describe it?
3 What furniture is there in the room?
4 What colour are the walls?
5 Are there other things in the room of a different colour?
6 What does he like doing in the room?

5   Think about your favourite room. Use the questions in Exercise 4 to help you. Make notes.

6   Write a description of your favourite room. Use 'My favourite room' and your notes from Exercise 5.

My favourite room

Paragraph 1
Introduce the room and give a general description.
My favourite room is .... . There's a .... .

Paragraph 2
Describe the furniture and walls.
The walls are .... and .... .

Paragraph 3
Say what you like doing in the room.
I like .... .

Remember!
• Use linking words *and, also, too, but, however.*
• Use the vocabulary in this unit.
• Check your grammar, spelling and punctuation.

Refresh Your Memory!

Grammar Review

1 **Complete the conversation with the correct form of the verbs.**

A What ¹ *are you reading* (you/read)?
B A postcard from my dad. He ² .... (work) in Paris at the moment, so we only ³ .... (see) him at weekends.
A ⁴ .... (he/like) Paris?
B Yes, he loves it. He ⁵ .... (look) for a new home for us there, but my mum doesn't want to go. All our friends and family ⁶ .... (live) here in London and she ⁷ .... (not speak) any French.
A ⁸ .... (you/speak) French?
B Well, we ⁹ .... (have) French lessons every day at school, but people in France always ¹⁰ .... (talk) very fast. I ¹¹ .... (not understand) very much!

2 **Complete the sentences with the correct form of these verbs.**

~~cook~~	eat	go	learn	live	not do
not listen	play	visit	watch		

1 My dad usually *cooks* our supper, but tonight we .... in a restaurant.
2 We .... about China in Geography at the moment. 1.3 billion people .... in China!
3 They .... to their new CD. They .... a film.
4 She .... judo on Thursdays. She .... volleyball.
5 I .... to school in Brighton, but today we .... a museum in London.

3 **Make sentences and questions.**

1 he / love / play / basketball
He loves playing basketball.
2 you / enjoy / run?
3 she / not mind / go / by bus
4 you / hate / lose
5 I / not like / learn / French
6 he / prefer / do / Computer Studies?
7 they / can't stand / listen / to rap music

Vocabulary Review

4 **Complete the sentences with the correct rooms and parts of the house.**

1 Come and have a drink on the *patio*. It's so sunny today.
2 The light on the l _ _ _ _ _ _ outside my bedroom doesn't work.
3 The dog usually sleeps under the table in the h _ _ _ .
4 The c _ _ _ _ _ _ in the attic is very low. I can't stand up in there.
5 There's a big mirror above the f _ _ _ _ _ _ _ _ .
6 When there isn't any rain, the grass on the l _ _ _ looks a bit brown.

5 **Match the beginnings (1–6) to the endings (a–f) of the sentences.**

1 There are flowers in the *f*
2 On the floor there's a
3 He went to bed and put his head on the
4 I woke up early because of my brother's
5 She loves looking at herself in the
6 That window needs a

a pillow.
b mirror.
c blind.
d alarm clock.
e rug.
f vase.

Speaking Review

6 ◉ 1.12 **Put the conversation in the correct order (1–6). Then listen and check.**

a Do you spend any time there?
b It's a bit small and it isn't very sunny.
c It's quite nice. It's got very big windows and some really comfortable armchairs.
d What's your balcony like? *1*
e No, I don't. I prefer sitting in the living room.
f What's that like?

Dictation

7 ◉ 1.13 **Listen and write in your notebook.**

✓ **My assessment profile:** Workbook page 127

Geography File

Houses around the world

1. Mongolia is near Russia and China in north-east Asia. The winters in Mongolia are very long and very cold. Many Mongolians keep horses. They move from place to place two or three times a year so their animals have enough food. When they move, their homes come with them. Their homes are called yurts and they must be strong because there are often winds of 160 km an hour.

2. The city of Hong Kong in the south of China is on a peninsula and two small islands. There are lots of mountains in Hong Kong, so there isn't a lot of space for houses. The buildings are very tall to save space. There are more tall buildings here than in any other city in the world. Forty percent of people live higher than the fourteenth floor! Most people live in really small apartments, but they don't mind. They often eat in restaurants and they don't spend a lot of time at home.

3. Belize is a small country in Central America. It is hot all year with a wet and a dry season. A lot of people live in stilt houses near the ocean. This type of house stays cool because the wind blows through it. It is also safer from snakes and other animals because it is not on the ground. People often leave their car under the house, out of the hot sun. From June to November, there are sometimes terrible storms, but the sea water doesn't come into the house.

Key Words

peninsula space stilt
blow ground

Reading

1. 🔊 1.14 Read about these homes. Match the photos (a–c) to the paragraphs (1–3).

2. 🔊 1.15 Listen to a description of another home. Choose the correct words to complete the fact file.

My Geography File

3. In groups, make a fact file about a home in another part of the world. Use the questions in Exercise 2 to help you.

4. Prepare a presentation for the class, including pictures or photos if possible. Then give your presentation.

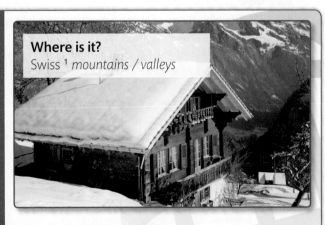

Where is it?
Swiss [1] *mountains / valleys*

What is the climate like?
[2] *warm / windy* in summer [3] *snowy / rainy* in winter

What is the home like? Why?
[4] *big / small* roof – protects the walls from bad weather
fireplace in the [5] *centre / back* of the house – keeps people warm
[6] *patio / balcony* – people can enjoy the sun in summer

2 What's The Story?

Grammar	Past simple; Past continuous; Past simple vs Past continuous
Vocabulary	Adjectives to describe pictures; Adjective + preposition
Speaking	Permission
Writing	A description of a picture

Vocabulary Adjectives to describe pictures

1 🔊 1.16 **Match** the photos (1–6) to the comments
(a–f). Check the meaning of the words in bold in a
dictionary. Then listen, check and repeat.

a It's an **interesting** photo of a famous place. It's
very **dramatic**.
b It's a **dull**, **silly** photo. I don't like it. *1*
c I love wildlife photos. This one is **dark**, but it's **lovely**.
d It's a bit **blurred**, but I like it. It's really **colourful**!
e It's obviously **fake** and it looks really **horrible**!
f The clothes are **old-fashioned**, but the photo
is **amusing**.

> Word list page 43 Workbook page 105

2 Complete the sentences with the adjectives in
Exercise 1.

1 My little brother is so *silly*. He's always telling jokes.
2 She often wears .... clothes. Red and green
T-shirts are her favourite.
3 My cat moved when I took this photo, so it's .... .
4 It's very .... in here. Can you turn on the light?
5 Everyone said the famous photo was .... .
Nobody thought it was real.
6 The storm last night was really .... – the sky was
purple! But I hate storms – I think they're .... .

3 In pairs, ask and answer about the photos.
Use the adjectives in Exercise 1.

Do you like photo 1?

*Yes, I do. I think it's .... and
..... What do you think?*

I disagree. I think it's .....

Brain Trainer Unit 2
Activity 2 Go to page 113

Reading

1 Look at the title of the magazine article and the photos. What do you think you are going to read about?

2 Read the article quickly and check your ideas.

3 Match the photos (a–c) to the paragraphs (1–3).

4 ◗) 1.17 Read the article again. Answer the questions.

1 What do the winners get?

The winners get a digital camera.

2 What is Lucas's photo of?
3 Where was Laine?
4 What is the weather like in Carrie's photo?
5 Does Click like Carrie's photo?
6 Does Jared like his photo?
7 Where were Jared and his family?

5 What about you? In pairs, ask and answer.

1 Do you take a lot of photos? What do you use – a camera or your mobile phone?
2 Did you take any photos on your last holiday? What were they like?
3 Describe the best photo you took last year.

CLICK! Magazine — young photographer competition

Every year at **CLICK!** Magazine, kids from all over the country send in photos for our fantastic competition. Here are this year's winners! The best photo in each category won a digital camera.

❶ People

Photographer: Lucas
Subject: My sister

Lucas says: On 5th August we were driving to France for our summer holiday. I took this picture of my sister, Laine, in the back of our car. It was a long drive and she wasn't enjoying it.

CLICK says: Lucas's photo is interesting and amusing. You can see his sister's thoughts in her face. What was she thinking? How was she feeling? This photo really tells a story.

❷ Places

Photographer: Carrie
Subject: A storm

Carrie says: Last month I was on holiday in Scotland with my family. There were a lot of storms and this was a very windy day! The grass and the trees were moving. The picture is a bit blurred, but I like it!

CLICK says: Carrie's picture is very dramatic. When you look at her picture, you can almost feel the wind!

❸ Animals

Photographer: Jared
Subject: On safari

Jared says: Last year I went on holiday to the Serengeti National Park. I was really stupid and I didn't have my camera, but I took a lot of photos with my mum's phone. This one is my favourite. It was 3 o'clock in the afternoon and it was raining. We weren't driving around, we were waiting for the rain to stop. That's when I saw the elephants.

CLICK says: This is a lovely photo!

Grammar Past simple

> Last year I went on holiday to the Serengeti National Park.
> I didn't have my camera.
> I took this picture of my sister, Laine.

> **Grammar reference** Workbook page 88

1 **Study the grammar table. Choose the correct option to complete the rule.**

> The Past simple describes *a finished action / an action in progress* in the past.

> We use the Past simple with past time adverbials, e.g. *yesterday, last week/year/Tuesday, two hours/days/weeks ago*, etc.

2 **Complete the sentences with the Past simple form of these verbs.**

get	not go	not play	~~see~~	take	watch

1 We *saw* the photo yesterday and we all thought it was fake.
2 They .... on holiday last year. They stayed at home.
3 .... you .... my email?
4 I .... football last weekend. I couldn't because the weather was horrible!
5 She .... a photo and put it on her blog a few minutes ago.
6 .... you .... the film last night? – Yes, we did. It was really dull!

3 **What about you? In pairs, ask and answer.**
1 What did you watch on TV yesterday?
2 Did you do any homework?
3 What did you do last weekend?
4 Did you take any photos of your friends?
5 Where did you go on holiday last year?
6 Did you have a good time?

> *What did you watch on TV yesterday?*

> *I watched the news.*

Past continuous

> On 5th August we were driving to France.
> We weren't driving around.
> What was she thinking?

> **Grammar reference** Workbook page 88

4 **Study the grammar table. Choose the correct option to complete the rule.**

> The Past continuous describes *a finished action / an action in progress* in the past.

5 **Complete the sentences with the Past continuous form of the verbs.**

1 I *was waiting* outside the cinema at 7 p.m. Luckily it .... . (wait/not rain)
2 At 9 o'clock last night they .... on the phone. They .... their homework. (talk/not do)
3 .... he .... football at 5 o'clock? No, he .... a match on TV. (play/watch)
4 At 8.30 a.m. she .... to school, she .... on a bus. (not cycle/sit)
5 What .... you .... on 1st January? .... you .... a party? (do/have)
6 At 1 o'clock I .... sandwiches, I .... pasta. (make/not cook)

6 **Read about a day in the life of a wildlife photographer. What was happening at different times of the day?**

1 9 o'clock / she / cook / breakfast
   At 9 o'clock she was cooking breakfast.
2 11 o'clock / they / look for / animals
3 1 o'clock / they / sit in the jeep
4 3 o'clock / she / take / photographs
5 5 o'clock / they / go back / home
6 7 o'clock / she / read / a book

Pronunciation Sentence stress

7a))) 1.18 **Listen and repeat.**

At <u>7</u> o'<u>clock</u> she was <u>reading</u> a <u>book</u>.

b))) 1.19 **Listen. Which words are stressed?**

1 What were you doing at 8 o'clock?
2 Were you watching TV?
3 He was doing his homework at 11 o'clock.
4 They weren't playing football after school.

c))) 1.19 **Listen and repeat.**

8 In pairs, ask and answer about yesterday.

What were you doing at 9 o'clock yesterday?

I was having a shower.

Vocabulary Adjective + preposition

1))) 1.20 **Look at these phrases. Check the meaning in a dictionary. Listen and repeat.**

afraid of	angry with	bad at	bored with
excited about	good at	interested in	keen on
popular with	proud of	sorry for	tired of

> **Word list** page 43 **Workbook** page 105

2 Match the beginnings (1–6) to the endings (a–f) of the sentences.

1 Karl is excited *f*
2 I'm afraid
3 He felt sorry
4 She was angry
5 Online videos are very popular
6 My brother is bad at

a with her brother because he told a lie.
b for Anna. She looked very sad.
c of snakes and spiders.
d with teenagers.
e Maths. I often help him with his homework.
f about the match tomorrow. He loves football!

3 Complete the text with the correct prepositions.

Are you interested ¹ *in* music? Are you keen ² ....
home videos? Well, there are lots of interesting video
clips online. Some are amusing and some are silly!
People's home videos are popular too, especially
pets doing funny things. So if you're good ³ ....
making home videos or you feel proud ⁴ .... a video
you made and want to share it, put it online. And
when you're bored ⁵ .... video clips and tired ⁶ ....
watching people doing silly things, just switch off your
computer and do something different!

4 **What about you?** In pairs, ask and answer.
1 Which school subjects are you interested in?
2 Which sports teams are popular with your friends?
3 What are you afraid of?
4 What achievement are you proud of?

Which school subjects are you interested in?

I'm really keen on History.

Brain Trainer Unit 2
Activity 3 Go to page 113

Chatroom Permission

Speaking and Listening

1 Look at the photo. Answer the questions.

   1 Where are the teenagers?
   2 Who are Ruby and Ash looking at?
   3 What do you think the attendant is saying?

2 🔊 1.21 Listen and read the conversation. Check your answers.

3 🔊 1.21 Listen and read again. Answer the questions.

   1 What did Ruby forget?

   She forgot her camera.

   2 What does Ash want to do?
   3 What can't you do in the museum?
   4 What can the teenagers do instead?
   5 Why does the attendant stop Ash?
   6 Where does Ruby decide to go?

4 Act out the conversation in groups of three.

Ash	Is this your camera, Ruby? You left it on the information desk.
Ruby	Yes, it is. Thanks!
Ash	Do you mind if I use it? My camera is broken. I was taking it out of its case when I dropped it.
Ruby	Of course I don't mind. Go ahead … , but can we take photos in the museum?
Ash	Let's ask. Excuse me, is it OK if we take photos?
Attendant	No, I'm afraid it isn't.
Ruby	That's a shame. I'm really interested in dinosaurs. But we can buy postcards. Look, there's a shop over there.
Ash	Great! I can buy some more crisps. This packet is empty.
Attendant	Excuse me. You can't eat in the exhibition hall, but there is a café near the entrance.
Ruby	We can get a drink there, too. Come on!

Say it in your language …
Go ahead.
That's a shame.

5 Look back at the conversation. How do Ash and Ruby ask for permission? How does the attendant refuse permission?

1 Do you .... if .... ? *Do you mind if I use it?*
2 ....OK if .... ?
3 No, I'm .... .

6 Read the phrases for asking for and giving or refusing permission.

Asking for permission	Giving or refusing permission
Can I/we .... ?	Yes, you can./ No, you can't.
Is it OK if I/we/ .... ?	Yes, of course./ No, I'm afraid it isn't.
Do you mind if I/we ... ?	No, I don't mind./ Yes, I do!/ Of course I don't mind.

7 🔊 1.22 **Listen to the conversations. Act out the conversations in pairs.**

Ella Can I ¹ stay up late tonight, Mum?
Mum No, you can't. You've got school tomorrow.
Tom Is it OK if I use ² your mobile phone? My phone isn't working.
Ash Sure. Here you are.
Ruby Do you mind if I ³ read your magazine?
Ella No, I don't mind.
Tom Do you mind if I ⁴ send a text message in class?
Teacher Yes, I do!

8 Work in pairs. Replace the words in purple in Exercise 7. Use these words and/or your own ideas. Act out the conversations.

> *Can I watch television, Mum?*
>
> *No, you can't. You've got school tomorrow.*

1 have a party / go out tonight / go to the cinema

2 your camera / your laptop / your MP3 player

3 watch TV / play a computer game / play the guitar

4 get to class late / don't do my homework / forget my books

Grammar   Past simple vs Past continuous

(long action)	(short action)
I was taking my camera out of its case	when I dropped it.

(short action)	(long action)
I dropped my camera	while I was taking it out of its case.

▷ **Grammar reference** Workbook page 88

1 **Study the grammar table. Choose the correct options to complete the rules.**

1 The Past continuous describes a *long / short* action in progress. The Past simple describes a *long / short* action. This can interrupt the long action.
2 We use *when / while* before a short action and *when / while* before a long action.

2 **Complete the sentences. Use the Past simple or Past continuous form of the verbs.**

1 We *were taking* (take) pictures when the museum attendant *stopped* (stop) us.
2 He .... (fall over) while he .... (skateboard).
3 She ... (do) her homework when her friend ... (arrive).
4 The doorbell .... (ring) while I .... (have) a bath.
5 We .... (eat) pizza when the film .... (start).
6 It .... (begin) to rain while they .... (walk) to school.

3 **Complete these sentences with your own ideas.**
1 I was watching a horror film when .... .
2 My friends were playing basketball when .... .
3 I was eating a burger when .... .
4 The lights went out while .... .
5 I heard a strange noise while .... .
6 We were sitting on the school bus when .... .

4 **Work in pairs. Ask and answer about your sentences in Exercise 3.**

> *What happened while you were watching a horror film?*
>
> *I saw a face at the window!*

Reading

1 Look at the photos. Answer the questions.

1 What can you see in the photos?
2 Where are the people?
3 What are they doing?

Great moments in history

This month *World Magazine* is looking at great moments in history. Do you remember these events? What about your parents or grandparents? What's the story behind the picture?

A V-J Day: 15th August 1945

Twenty-seven-year-old Edith Shain was working as a nurse in New York when she heard the news on the radio – the war* was over! All across the USA, people were celebrating. Edith was celebrating in Times Square when a sailor kissed her. Edith didn't know the sailor, but she wasn't angry with him. A young photographer was in Times Square, too. He took this photo. A week later Edith saw the photo in *Life* magazine. She was surprised, but she was also proud of the photo!

2 Read the magazine article quickly and check your answers to Exercise 1.

3 🔊 1.23 **Read the article again. Copy the table and complete the information.**

	A	B	C
Event?	V-J Day	....	World Cup Final
When?	....	20th July 1969	....
Where?	....	....	Mexico
Who?	Edith Shain	....	....

4 🔊 1.23 **Read the article again. Answer the questions.**

Paragraph A

1 Why did Edith go to Times Square?
2 How did she feel about the sailor?
3 How did she find out about the photo?

Paragraph B

4 Why was the event on TV important?
5 What did Aldrin and Armstrong do on the Moon?

Paragraph C

6 Why was the 1970 World Cup Final special for Pelé?
7 What was different about this sports event?

B Man on the Moon: 20th July 1969

Half a billion people were watching an important event on television. What were they watching? Astronauts Neil Armstrong and Buzz Aldrin. Armstrong was the first man to walk on the Moon. 'That's one small step for man, one giant leap for mankind,' he said. The two astronauts stayed on the Moon for twenty-one hours and collected samples for scientists back on Earth. They left an American flag and some footprints. The flag and the footprints are still there today!

C FIFA World Cup Final: 21st June 1970

More than 100,000 people were waiting in Mexico's Azteca football stadium. Italy were playing Brazil in the World Cup Final and Pelé was in the Brazilian team. After the match, a photographer took this picture. It was Pelé's third World Cup win and the first major sporting event to appear on TV in colour. Millions of people were watching when Pelé lifted the trophy in his yellow football shirt!

* The Second World War (1939–45)

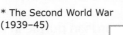

Key Words
sailor   kissed   event   leap
mankind   stadium   trophy

Listening

1 Look at the famous photo on page 118. Answer the questions.

1 What can you see in the photo?
2 When do you think the event happened? 1920s, 1930s, 1950s?

2 🔊 1.24 **Listen to two people talking about the photo and check your answers to Exercise 1.**

🔊 **Listening Bank Unit 2** page 118

Writing   A description of a picture

1   Read the Writing File.

> **Writing File**   Describing a picture
>
> When you describe a picture or a photo, use these words and phrases to say where things are:
> - in the foreground
> - in the background
> - in the centre/middle of the picture
> - on the left/right
> - in the left/right-hand corner

in the middle of the picture   in the background

in the foreground   on the left   on the right   in the right-hand corner

2   Read the description. Find four words and phrases that say where things are.

My favourite photo by Jamie

I took this photo on my mobile phone last month. It's of a family day out with my parents, my sisters, Tara and Marie and my cousin, Joe. We took our dog, Spot with us and Joe brought his dog, Rex. The house in the background is Blenheim Palace. It's a bit blurred, but it looks dramatic!

Joe and Rex are on the right of the picture. Rex was excited about some birds in a tree. He was barking and Joe was telling him to be quiet. Marie and Tara were laughing because Rex wasn't listening. That's Spot in the foreground of the picture and Mum and Dad are in the background. Dad was taking a video with his new video camera. I like this photo because it's amusing. You can see how everyone feels – especially Rex!

3   Look at Jamie's photo. Are the sentences true (T) or false (F)?

1   There is a dog in the left-hand corner. *F*
2   There are two people in the centre of the picture.
3   There's a palace in the background.
4   There's a man with a video camera on the right.
5   There's a small dog in the foreground.
6   There's a girl on the left.

4   Read the description again. Answer the questions.

1   Where were Jamie and his family?
    They were at Blenheim Palace.
2   When did they go there?
3   Why was Rex barking?
4   Why were Marie and Tara laughing?
5   What was Jamie's dad doing?
6   Why does Jamie like the photo?

5   Choose an interesting photo of your family or friends. Ask yourself these questions. Make notes.

1   Where is it?
2   Why were you there?
3   Who/What is in the photo?
4   Where are the different people in the photo?
5   What were they doing?
6   Why do you like the photo?

6   Write a description of your favourite picture or photo. Use 'My favourite photo' and your notes from Exercise 5.

> **My favourite photo**
>
> **1** Introduction: where, when and who
> *I took this photo* .... (when?). *I was* .... (where?) .... (who with?) .... .
> **2** Description
> - what you can see in the photo
> .... *is on the right of the picture and* .....
> *In the background there is/are* .... .
> - what the people were doing
> *My parents/brother/cousin was/were* .... .
> **3** Conclusion: Why you like the photo

 Remember!
- Say where things and people are in your photo.
- Say what people were doing.
- Use the vocabulary in this unit.
- Check your grammar, spelling and punctuation.

Refresh Your Memory!

Grammar Review

1 Complete the sentences with the Past simple form of these verbs.

go	~~have~~	make	not do	not write	see	send

1 *Did* they *have* their English lesson this morning?
2 I .... you a text message five minutes ago.
3 We .... to the cinema last weekend.
4 I .... my homework last night. I was very tired.
5 .... you .... some sandwiches for lunch?
6 She .... her blog last weekend. She didn't have time.
7 He .... a dramatic photo in the newspaper yesterday.

2 Complete the story with the Past continuous form of the verbs.

It was 4.30 p.m. and I ¹ *was sitting* (sit) on the school bus with my friend Emma. We ² .... (not talk) because Emma ³ .... (read) a magazine. I ⁴ .... (look) out of the window. It ⁵ .... (rain) and people ⁶ .... (walk) along the street. A girl and a boy ⁷ .... (stand) near the bus stop and they ⁸ .... (laugh). The boy ⁹ .... (not carry) an umbrella and his hair was wet. He ¹⁰ .... (hold) the girl's hand. I recognised the boy – it was Emma's boyfriend! Then I looked at Emma. She ¹¹ .... (not read) her magazine, she ¹² .... (look) out of the window and she ¹³ .... (not smile).

3 Choose the correct options.

Ben I ¹ *called / was calling* you last night. Where were you?
Nina I was at home all evening. What time ² *did you call / were you calling*?
Ben At 8 o'clock. The phone ³ *rang / ringing* for a long time!
Nina That's funny. I ⁴ *didn't hear / wasn't hearing* it.
Ben ⁵ *Did you sleep / Were you sleeping*?
Nina No, I wasn't. I wasn't tired!
Ben Then what ⁶ *did you do / were you doing*?
Nina Ah, I remember. I ⁷ *listened / was listening* to some music on my MP3 player.

Vocabulary Review

4 Correct the sentences. Use these words.

colourful	dark	~~fake~~	horrible
interesting	old-fashioned	silly	

1 That's a cheap diamond ring. It's probably **real**. *fake*
2 I love wildlife photos. They're often really **boring**.
3 Matt was **lovely** to Sue. He really upset her.
4 It's six o'clock in the evening. It's already **light** outside.
5 It's **sensible** to ride a bike without a helmet.
6 My grandmother's apartment is very **modern**.
7 That's a really **dull** picture. I love the bright colours.

5 Complete the sentences with these adjectives.

afraid	angry	bad	bored
~~excited~~	interested	popular	tired

1 Paolo is very *excited* about his holiday.
2 They were .... with the TV show. It was really dull.
3 I'm .... at Maths. I never get good marks for my homework.
4 Magazines are always .... with girls.
5 Guess what?! Joel is .... of mice!
6 Are you .... in football?
7 I'm .... of homework. There's too much to do.
8 I was .... with my brother because he ate my pizza.

Speaking Review

6))) 1.25 **Put the conversation in the correct order (1–6). Then listen and check.**

a Can I have a party on my birthday? *1*
b Yes, I do! It's very expensive!
c Do you mind if I take the whole class?
d No, it isn't. You can go to a pizzeria.
e Great! Is it OK if I have the party at home, with my friends?
f Hmm … OK. Yes, you can.

Dictation

7))) 1.26 **Listen and write in your notebook.**

 My assessment profile: Workbook page 128

⊗ Kieron Williamson's Profile

👤 **Age:**
10 years old

Home country:
United Kingdom

My favourite things …

painting, football, watching TV, computer games

Reading

1 **Read Kieron's profile. Complete the sentences.**

1 Kieron comes from …. .
2 He's …. old.
3 He likes playing …. and …. .

2 🔊 **1.27** **Read the article. Answer the questions.**

1 Which artists is Kieron sometimes compared to?
   Picasso and Matisse.
2 Who does he live with?
3 How old was he when he started painting?
4 What was his first painting of?
5 How did his paintings change?
6 Who helped him develop his hobby?
7 What are his paintings like?
8 How much are Kieron's pictures?

Kieron's paintings

Young artist

He's a famous English artist. He is in the newspapers and on TV and all the tickets for his last exhibition sold out in fourteen minutes! He's called the new 'Picasso', or the 'mini-Matisse' and he's only ten years old. Meet Kieron Williamson.

Kieron was born in 2002 in a town in the south-east of England. He lives with his mum, dad and little sister, Billie-Jo. Kieron is a typical boy. He's good at computer games and he watches TV, he's interested in football and he likes riding his bike. He's also a brilliant artist. It all started on a family holiday when he was five years old. He was playing on the beach when he saw some boats. He asked his parents for a drawing pad and the next day he began to draw pictures of them. At first his drawings weren't great, but then he started to add background scenery, hills and houses. His pictures got better and better and he began to ask his parents for advice. Kieron's mum and dad are not artists, so they asked a local artist for help. She gave Kieron lessons and in August 2009, he had his first exhibition.

Kieron works hard at his art. He gets up at 6 a.m. every morning and paints. His pictures are of the countryside around his town. They're dramatic and colourful and he paints four or five every week. People all over the world love Kieron's paintings – and lots of people are collecting them, so they now cost more than £1,000 each.

Key Words

exhibition   sold out   drawing pad
scenery   countryside

Class discussion

1 Do you know any famous artists from your country?
2 How old were they when they started painting?
3 Do you know any paintings by Picasso or Matisse? What are they like?

3 It's A Bargain!

Grammar	Comparatives and superlatives; *too* and *enough; much, many, a lot of*
Vocabulary	Shopping nouns; Money verbs
Speaking	Asking for help
Writing	A customer review

Vocabulary   Shopping nouns

1   1.28   **Match the pictures (1–15) to these words. Then listen, check and repeat.**

bargain	cashpoint	change	coin
customer	high street	market stall	note
price	products	queue	sale
shop assistant	shopping basket *1*	stallholder	

> **Word list** page 43   **Workbook** page 106

2   **Complete the conversation with the words in Exercise 1.**

Dean This is my favourite shop on the [1] *high street*.
Louis I love this coat, but how much is it?
Dean Ask the [2] .... . She'll know.
Louis Oh! It's £17. It's half price in the [3] .... .
Dean It's a [4] .... ! Are you going to buy it?
Louis Yes, but I must go to the [5] .... first. I've only got a twenty pence [6] .... and I can't buy a coat with that!
Dean But there's always a long [7] .... at the cashpoint. Here's a twenty pound [8] .... . You can get some money later.

3   **Complete the sentences with the words in Exercise 1.**

1 The *price* of petrol is very high.
2 Lucy makes T-shirts and sells them at a .... on Saturdays. She knows all the other .... .
3 This shop sells really good .... – they often buy from the local farmers.
4 Shop assistants should always make sure they give the .... the correct .... when they buy something.

4   **In pairs, ask and answer about your local area.**

1 Where or when are there good bargains?
2 Which shops have friendly shop assistants?
3 Where or when are there often queues?

Brain Trainer Unit 3
Activity 2 Go to page 113

Reading

1 **Look at the photos. Do you think these sentences are true (T) or false (F)?**

1 The market is very old. *T*
2 These days, it's only popular with old people.
3 It sells fresh food.
4 The prices are expensive.

2 🔊 **1.29** **Read the magazine article and check your answers to Exercise 1.**

3 **Read the article again. Match the headings (A–D) to the paragraphs (1–4).**

A The market has a long history.
B Today, that is difficult to believe.
C Shopping is often more interesting at the market, too.
D The award is no surprise to Spitalfields' stallholders. *1*

4 **Answer the questions.**

1 What did Spitalfields Market win?
   The title of 'Best Market' in the British Market Awards.
2 Is it easy to have a stall at the market?
3 What did people buy at Spitalfields Market before the 1990s?
4 Why did people think the market had no future?
5 What does Nick like about the products at the market?
6 What is good about the food at the market?
7 Why doesn't Diyanah like shopping in the town centre?

5 **What about you?** **Answer the questions.**

1 What are the markets like in your area?
2 How often do you go to a market?
3 What do you buy there?
4 What do you like/dislike about markets?

News | London

London Market Wins Award

Spitalfields has won the title of 'Best Market' in the British Market Awards.

1 .... 'This is the most fashionable market in Britain!' says Vicky Green at her bag stall. 'It's popular with lots of famous people. Every stallholder in London wants to be here, but there isn't enough space for everyone.'

2 .... For hundreds of years, it was the best place to buy fruit and vegetables in London. But by the 1990s, the fruit and vegetable stalls were too big for the small market area at Spitalfields. The stalls moved to a bigger market further from the centre of London. A lot of people thought that Spitalfields Market had no future.

3 .... It now has hundreds of stalls, with everything from Indian scarves to African drums, from fresh bread to designer jeans. And customers love it. 'Prices here  are often cheaper than in shops, so you can find some great bargains,' explains Nick Baines, 16. Others come to the market for the quality of its food. 'Supermarket food isn't fresh enough,' says Kath Manning, 40. 'The food here is better because it comes from local farms and the stallholders are friendlier than shop assistants.'

4 .... 'In every high street in Britain, you find the same shops with the same products,' says Diyanah Chowdray, 21. 'I prefer Spitalfields because the stalls here change every week and you can't buy their products anywhere else.'

For Spitalfields and other markets like it, the future has never looked better.

Grammar Comparatives and superlatives

Adjective	Comparative	Superlative
cheap	cheaper	cheapest
nice	nicer	nicest
big	bigger	biggest
friendly	friendlier	friendliest
interesting	more interesting	most interesting
good	better	best
bad	worse	worst
far	further	furthest

Stallholders are friendlier than shop assistants.
Spitalfields is the most fashionable market in Britain!

Grammar reference Workbook page 90

1 Study the grammar table and the examples.
Complete the rules with *comparative* or *superlative*.

> **1** We compare two people or things with the .... .
> **2** We compare one person or thing to the rest of its group with the .... .
> **3** We use *the* before the .... .
> **4** We use *than* after the .... .

2 Complete the sentences with the correct form of the adjectives.
1 We're *hungrier* (hungry) than you.
2 August is the .... (hot) month of the year.
3 It is the .... (large) market in Britain.
4 The T-shirt is .... (clean) than the jacket.
5 My sister's .... (selfish) than my brother.
6 This is the .... (bad) day of my life!

3 Complete the text with the correct form of the adjectives.

The ¹ *most popular* (popular) markets in Thailand are on water and the stalls are boats. Taling Chan is the ² .... (good) market near the city of Bangkok, but the ³ .... (big) and ⁴ .... (busy) market in Thailand is at Ratchaburi. It is ⁵ .... (far) from Bangkok than Taling Chan and prices there are ⁶ .... (expensive) than prices in other places. Why? Because this market is one of the ⁷ .... (famous) and ⁸ .... (exciting) markets in the world!

too and *enough*

> The jeans are too expensive.
> The jeans aren't cheap enough.
> I haven't got enough money for the jeans.

Grammar reference Workbook page 90

4 Study the grammar table. Complete the rules with *too* or *enough*.

> **1** We use .... + adjective.
> **2** We use *(not)* adjective + ...
> **3** We use .... + noun.

5 Make sentences and questions.
1 aren't / people / There / enough
   There aren't enough people.
2 you / too / tired / Are / ?
3 fast / enough / It / isn't
4 never / food / enough / eats / She
5 clever / I'm / enough / not
6 She / too / works / always / hard

6 Complete the second sentence so it means the same as the first. Use the word in brackets.
1 That colour is too bright. (dark)
   That colour *isn't dark enough*.
2 The shopping basket is too heavy. (light)
   The shopping basket .... .
3 The film wasn't exciting enough for me. (boring)
   The film .... for me.
4 Our football team is too small. (players)
   We haven't got .... in our football team.
5 The library is never quiet enough. (noisy)
   The library is always .... .

7 **What about you?** Make sentences about different shops, shopping areas or markets where you live. Use comparatives, superlatives, *too* and *enough*. Use some of these adjectives.

big	busy	cheap	cool
expensive	good	interesting	noisy
old	quiet	small	

> *The shopping centre is too busy on Saturdays.*

> *There aren't enough clothes shops in the town centre.*

Vocabulary Money verbs

1 🔊 1.30 **Match the pictures (1–12) to these verb pairs. Then listen, check and repeat.**

buy/sell *1–2*	cost/afford
lend/borrow	pay in cash/pay by credit card
save/spend	win/earn

Word list page 43 **Workbook** page 106

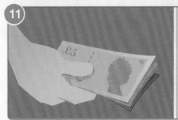 

2 **Complete the sentences with the correct verbs.**

borrow/lend	~~cost/afford~~	in cash/by credit card
saved/spent	sells/buys	won/earns

1 The DVDs *cost* £12. I can't *afford* one. I haven't got enough money.
2 The stallholder .... fruit and vegetables. The customer .... her fruit from him.
3 Sam took out a note from his wallet and paid for the sandwiches .... . Ellie didn't have any cash so she paid for her lunch .... .
4 They sometimes .... their dad's laptop. But he doesn't always .... it to them.
5 Tara .... her money in the bank, so she's got £500 now. Tod .... all his money on computer games, so he hasn't got any money now.
6 Daniel .... £100 in a competition last week. Olivia only .... £100 in a week.

Pronunciation /ɒ/ and /əʊ/

3a 🔊 1.31 **Listen and repeat.**

/ɒ/	/əʊ/
cost	go
long	note
shop	show

b 🔊 1.32 **Listen and repeat. Then practise saying the sentences.**

1 Go home on the boat.
2 The shops don't close at six o'clock.
3 Can I borrow your orange coat?
4 The stallholder sold me some old posters.
5 The queue at the post office is so slow.

4 **Match the beginnings (1–5) to the endings (a–e) of the sentences.**

1 My favourite shop sells   a save for it.
2 I usually spend my money   b by credit card.
3 I sometimes borrow money   c pet snakes.
4 I usually pay for new clothes   d from my dad.
5 If I can't afford something nice, I   e on DVDs.

5 **Look at the sentence beginnings (1–5) in Exercise 4. Complete the sentences so they are true for you.**

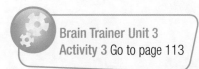
Brain Trainer Unit 3
Activity 3 Go to page 113

Chatroom Asking for help

Speaking and Listening

1 **Look at the photo. What does Ella want to buy?**

2))) 1.33 **Listen and read the conversation. Check your answer.**

3))) 1.33 **Listen and read again. Answer the questions.**

   1 What help does Tom give Ella?

   He helps her with her bags.

   2 Why does Ella want the T-shirt?

   3 When does Ella want to buy the T-shirt?

   4 Can the shop assistant save the T-shirt for Ella?

   5 Why does Ella ask Tom about his money?

   6 Does Tom think the T-shirt is a bargain?

4 **Act out the conversation in groups of three.**

Ella	Hey, Tom. **Can you give me a hand with** these bags?
Tom	Sure.
Ella	Thanks. I want to look at these T-shirts.
Tom	But you've got a lot of T-shirts, Ella. You don't need a new one.
Ella	I haven't got many nice T-shirts. These are nicer than all my clothes at home. Oh look, there's the shop assistant … Excuse me, **would you mind saving** this for me until next week?
Assistant	Sorry, I can't. It's against the rules.
Ella	That's a shame. Er, Tom … how much money have you got?
Tom	Why?
Ella	Well, I can't afford any new clothes at the moment. **Could you lend** me some money?
Tom	No problem. How much?
Ella	£20.
Tom	£20 is too much money for one T-shirt!
Ella	But for £20 I can buy five T-shirts.
Tom	Oh, Ella! You're impossible!

Say it in your language …
It's against the rules.
You're impossible!

5 Look back at the conversation. Complete the sentences.

1 Can you *give me a hand* with these bags?
2 .... saving this for me until next week?
3 .... lend me some money?

6 Read the phrases for asking for help. Find three responses in the conversation.

Asking for help	Responding
Could you … ?	OK.
Can you …?	Sure.
Can/Could you give me a hand with …?	No problem.
Would you mind …-*ing*?	Sorry, I can't.

7 🔊 1.34 **Listen to the conversations. Does each person agree to help or not? Act out the conversations in pairs.**

Ruby Can you lend me [1] a pen?
Ella Sorry, I can't. I've only got one.

Ash Could you give me a hand with [2] this homework?
Ruby Sorry, I can't.

Ella Would you mind [3] carrying my bag?
Tom No problem.

8 Work in pairs. Replace the words in purple in Exercise 7. Use these words and/or your own ideas. Act out the conversations.

Can you lend me a calculator?
Sorry, I can't. I've only got one.

1 a pencil / a ruler / a rubber

2 my English / these sandwiches / this computer

3 taking a photo / opening the door / coming with me

Grammar   *much, many, a lot of*

How much money has she got?	How many T-shirts has she got?
She's got a lot of money.	She's got a lot of T-shirts.
She hasn't got much/a lot of money.	She hasn't got many/a lot of T-shirts.
She's got too much money.	She's got too many T-shirts.

Grammar reference Workbook page 90

1 Study the grammar table. Complete the rules with *(too) much, (too) many* or *a lot of*.

1 With countable nouns, we use *a lot of* or .... .
2 With uncountable nouns, we use *a lot of* or .... .
3 In affirmative sentences, we usually use .... .
4 In negative sentences, we can use .... , ... or .... .

2 Choose the correct options.

1 There are too *much / many* people here.
2 He doesn't earn *much / many* money.
3 She does *a lot of / much* homework every night.
4 How *much / many* credit cards have you got?
5 I ate too *much / many* food yesterday.
6 He took *a lot of / many* photos.

3 Complete the text with *much, many* or *a lot of*.

How [1] *many* underground shops are there in your city? In Toronto, Canada, there are 1,200! In winter there's [2] .... snow in Toronto and people don't spend [3] .... time outside in the cold. In summer, there are too [4] .... cars on the streets and too [5] .... pollution. So, instead, [6] .... people like shopping on the 28 km of paths under the city.

4 In pairs, ask and answer about these things.

cash in your purse or wallet	free time	homework
shoes	T-shirts	

How much free time do you have?
I have a lot of free time.

Reading

1 Look at the heading and the photos. What connection do you think the photos have to the text?

The internet

← → C ♠

The internet – the world's biggest market

1 .... A lot of people find shopping online easier than going to their local high street or to the supermarket and they love the cheaper prices on the internet. They also like reading other customers' reviews, so they know different people's opinions about a

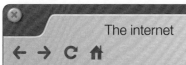

product before they buy. But for many people, the most important advantage of online shopping is the choice.

2 .... Shopping in your town isn't easy if you don't like the same things as everyone else. But that isn't a problem online. On the internet your shopping centre is the world. You can buy from a Korean music shop, a Mexican chilli farmer and a Nigerian hat designer all in one afternoon.

3 .... The internet is also the perfect place to find something strange or unusual. You can buy a jar of Alaskan snow, the poster for a 1920s horror film or a potato in the shape of a rabbit! Soon after singer Justin Bieber went to the hairdresser, a fan bought a small box of his hair at an auction website for $40,668!

4 .... For some people, experiences are more important than possessions and they too can find a lot of interesting things on the internet. Would you like to give your name to a character in a novel or appear in a TV show? Win the right online auction and you can. In 2008, someone even bought an evening with actress Scarlett Johannson for $40,100 (the money went to the charity Oxfam). You don't get much exercise when you shop online and you don't see many friendly faces, but if you are looking for something unusual, there's nowhere better!

Key Words

advantage	fan	auction
character	novel	charity

2 Read the text quickly and check your ideas.

3 🔊 1.35 Read the text again. Match the headings (A–D) to the paragraphs (1–4).

A An experience to remember
B International shopping
C Why shop online? *1*
D No one else has that!

4 Read the text again. Answer the questions.

1 How do online shoppers know if other customers like a product? *They read their reviews.*
2 Why is it difficult for some people to find nice things in their town?
3 Why did someone pay $40,668 for a box of hair?
4 How, according to the text, can the internet help you to be on TV?
5 How did Scarlett Johannson help Oxfam?
6 What two disadvantages of online shopping does the text mention?

5 In pairs, compare shopping on the internet and shopping on your local high street.

How much do you buy on the internet?

I buy about two things online every month.

Listening

1 What problems do people sometimes have when they buy things online? Make a list.

2 🔊 1.36 Listen to the news report. Was the boy's problem one of the things on your list in Exercise 1?

🔊 Listening Bank Unit 3 page 118

Writing A customer review

1 Read the Writing File.

Writing File Expressing opinion

You can introduce your opinion with:

I think (that) those boots are a waste of money.
I don't think (that) it's a very useful bag.
In my opinion, it's too expensive.
I find it very difficult to use.

2 Read a customer's online review of a camera. Find three phrases that express an opinion.

Search: digital camera

iPix S70 Blue **£90** ☆☆☆☆☆

Other colours available ■ ■ ■ ■ ■ ■

Your reviews ↘

The iPix S70 camera costs £90 in the sale. It comes in a choice of six different colours.
The camera is only 10 cm long and it's very light, so it goes in a small bag easily. It takes great photos inside and outside and it can make short videos, too. I find it very easy to use.
However, it has some problems. When you take a photo of something too near to the camera, the quality of the photo isn't very good. Another problem is the size of the screen. It isn't big enough if you want to look at your photos on the camera. In my opinion, the iPix S70 isn't the best small camera in the shops. However, at £90, I think it's a good bargain.

3 Complete the sentences with these phrases.

| I don't think | I find it | I think | In my opinion |

1 I love this book. .... very interesting.
2 I really don't want that poster. .... that it's very nice.
3 I never go there. .... , it's the worst shop in town.
4 .... , markets sell the freshest food.

4 Read the review again and answer the questions.

1 How much does the camera cost?
   It costs £90 in the sale.
2 Is there a choice (e.g. of size, colour, etc.)?
3 Is its size a good thing or a bad thing? Why?
4 What can you do with it?
5 Is it easy to use?
6 What problems does it have?
7 What is the writer's general opinion of it?

5 You are going to write a customer review of one of these products: a mobile phone, an MP3 player or a bag. Use the questions in Exercise 4 to help you. Make notes.

6 Write your customer review. Use 'My review' and your notes from Exercise 5.

My review

Paragraph 1
Introduce the product. Say how much it costs and what choices there are (colour, size, etc.)

Paragraph 2
Describe the product. Say what you like about it.

Paragraph 3
Describe any problems with the product.

Paragraph 4
Summarise your opinion of the product.

Remember!
- Express opinions with expressions from the Writing File.
- Use the vocabulary and grammar you've practised in this unit.
- Check your grammar, spelling and punctuation.

Refresh Your Memory!

Grammar Review

1 Make eight sentences comparing the shops in the table. Use the comparative or superlative form of these adjectives.

bad	big	cheap	expensive
~~friendly~~	good	large	~~popular~~

	Pound Stop	Fashionista	Mason's
Size	2000 m²	900 m²	3500 m²
Prices	Everything £1	£2–£90	£30–£20,999
Customers per week	5000	12,000	2000
Shop Assistants	unfriendly	very friendly	friendly
Products	not very good	OK	very good

Fashionista is the most popular shop.

Mason's has got friendlier shop assistants than Pound Stop.

2 Make sentences.

1 hasn't / She / enough / friends / got
   She hasn't got enough friends.
2 enough / T-shirt / The / big / isn't
3 The / too / expensive / are / scarves
4 is / market / too / The / noisy
5 money / don't / enough / We / earn
6 aren't / enough / My / fashionable / clothes

3 Complete the conversation with *a lot of, much* or *many*.

A I haven't got ¹ *many* summer clothes, so I'm going shopping.
B Oh, I need ² .... things in town. Can I give you a list? I can't go with you because I've got too ³ .... homework.
A OK, if you're quick. I haven't got ⁴ .... time. There's a bus in five minutes and you know there aren't ⁵ .... buses at the weekend.
B Thanks. Here's the list. I hope there aren't too ⁶ .... things.
A What? How ⁷ .... hands do you think I've got?! I can't carry all this!

Vocabulary Review

4 Match these words to the definitions (1–6).

bargain	~~cashpoint~~	coin
customer	sale	shopping basket

1 You use a card to get money from this. *cashpoint*
2 This type of money is small and hard.
3 You put the products you want to buy in a supermarket in this.
4 When a shop has this, the prices are cheaper.
5 This person buys things in shops.
6 This is a product with a cheap price.

5 One of the underlined words in each sentence is incorrect. Correct it.

1 'How much do the jeans ~~spend~~?' *cost* 'Ten pounds. They're a very good price.'
2 He wins a lot of money on his market stall because he sells really popular things.
3 Do you want to pay in cash or with credit card?
4 He can't cost designer clothes on the high street in his town.
5 Can I lend a ten pound note so I can buy my train ticket?
6 She won the lottery and spent all the money in the bank.

Speaking Review

6))) 1.37 Complete the conversations with these words. Then listen and check.

can	~~could~~	give	mind
problem	sorry	sure	with

A ¹ *Could* you lend me your mobile phone for a minute, please?
B ² .... . Here you are.
A Would you ³ .... carrying the shopping basket?
B OK. No ⁴ .... .
A ⁵ .... you ⁶ .... me a hand ⁷ .... the food?
B ⁸ .... , I can't. I'm too busy.

Dictation

7))) 1.38 Listen and write in your notebook.

My assessment profile: Workbook page 129

Maths File

Price of products across the world

Do you pay more for products than people in other countries? Look at this table and find out.

	The UK	China	The USA	France
ADMIT ONE	£8.00 (€…)	¥30 (€…)	$9.00 (€…)	€6.20
(burger)	£2.20 (€…)	¥14.50 (€…)	$3.60 (€…)	€3.50
(magazine)	£3.50 (€…)	¥5 (€…)	$3.50 (€…)	€2.40
(trainers)	£60.00 (€…)	¥388 (€…)	$55.00 (€…)	€50.00

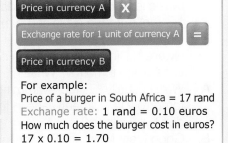

Do the Maths

Do you know how to change one currency into another? Use our easy guide.
First, you must know the exchange rate. Exchange rates change every day. You can find them online or in a newspaper or in banks and post offices.
Then do the Maths.

> Price in currency A **X**
> Exchange rate for 1 unit of currency A **=**
> Price in currency B

For example:
Price of a burger in South Africa = 17 rand
Exchange rate: 1 rand = 0.10 euros
How much does the burger cost in euros?
17 x 0.10 = 1.70
The burger costs 1.70 euros.

Key Words

currency   exchange rate

Reading

1 Match the currencies to the countries. What is your country's currency?

> pound (£)   dollar ($)
> yuan (¥)   euro (€)
> rand (R)

> China
> France
> South Africa
> The UK
> The USA

2 Read the magazine article and answer the questions.
   1 How much do trainers cost in the UK? £60.00
   2 In which country is a magazine more expensive than a burger?
   3 How many magazines can you buy for the price of a cinema ticket in China?
   4 Name two places where you can find out about exchange rates.

3 Calculate the price in euros of the items from the UK, China and the USA in the table in the article. Use the exchange rates below.

EXCHANGE RATES	
£1	€1.20
¥1	€0.10
US$1	€0.75

4 🔊 1.39 Listen. Are these sentences true (T) or false (F)? Use your euro prices from Exercise 3 to help you.

My Maths File

5 Find out the price of three items in your country and in two other countries with a different currency. Convert the prices into your currency.

6 Make a poster with the information from Exercise 5. Include a table like the one in the article and sentences comparing the items.

Switzerland has the most expensive coffee. Tickets to football matches are cheaper in Mexico than in my country.

Review

Grammar   Present simple and continuous

1 Complete the conversation with the Present simple or Present continuous form of the verbs.

A [1] *Do* you *want* (want) to come out with us tonight? We [2] .... (go) to Pat's house after her music lesson. You know she [3] .... (have) a music lesson at 5 p.m. on Fridays. Then we [4] .... (go) out for a pizza at 6 p.m.

B Oh, I [5] .... (play) a tennis match at that time. We always [6] .... (have) matches on Friday nights. But I'm free tomorrow. What [7] .... you .... ? (do)

A Well, I usually [8] .... (go) swimming, but tomorrow I [9] .... (meet) Jane in town. Why don't you join us?

B Good idea. My mum [10] .... (drive) me into town for shopping anyway, so I can meet you afterwards.

Verb + -ing

2 Make sentences.

1 Do / you like / get up / early?
   Do you like getting up early?
2 I / prefer / watch films to plays.
3 Jenny / hate / do housework.
4 My mum / really enjoy / work in the garden.
5 I / not mind / tidy / my room. But I / hate / iron.
6 My dad / not like / lie / on the beach.

Past simple

3 Complete the conversation with the Past simple form of the verbs.

A What [1] *did* you *do* (do) at the weekend?
B I [2] .... (go) shopping.
A What [3] .... you .... ? (buy)
B I [4] .... (buy) a birthday present for my friend. She [5] .... (have) a party on Saturday night.
A [6] .... (be) it a good party?
B Yes! Her brother's band [7] .... (play) and we all [8] .... (dance). I [9] .... (give) her a CD and we [10] .... (listen) to that as well.
A What time [11] .... the party .... ? (finish)
B I [12] .... (come) home at about 11 p.m. But I think the party only [13] .... (end) at midnight!

Past continuous

4 Complete the text with the Past continuous forms of the verbs.

Yesterday, everyone in our house [1] *was doing* (do) something different. My brother and his friends [2] .... (play) football in the garden. My dad [3] .... (fix) his bike. My mum [4] .... (make) a cake and [5] .... (listen) to the radio. And me? I [6] .... (lie) on my bed and [7] .... (read) my favourite magazine! What [8] .... you .... ? (do)

Past simple v Past continuous

5 Choose the correct option.

1 I *was texting / texted* my friend while I *was walking / walked* down the street. Then I *was walking / walked* into a tree!
2 We *were watching / watched* a film on TV when suddenly it *stopped / was stopping* working. So we *weren't seeing / didn't see* the end of the film.
3 It *was raining / rained* yesterday so we *weren't having / didn't have* a picnic.
4 While I *was waiting / waited* at the dentist, I *was reading / read* magazines.
5 I *was sitting / sat* in a café when I suddenly *was seeing / saw* an old friend.
6 I *was hurting / hurt* my ankle yesterday. I *was standing / stood* on a chair to reach the top shelf when I *was falling / fell off*.

Comparatives and superlatives

6 Make sentences using the correct form of the adjectives.

1 A whale / heavy / an elephant.
   A whale is heavier than an elephant.
2 The cheetah is / fast / animal in the world.
3 Which is / big – London or Paris?
4 I think Adam Sandler is / funny / actor in Hollywood.
5 That was / good / pizza / in the world!
6 My Maths test was / bad / my English test.
7 Tracey lives / far / from school / me.
8 The weather today is / good / yesterday.
9 Do you think French is / easy / English?
10 In summer the beach is / crowded / in winter.

too and enough

7 Complete the second sentence so that it means the same as the first. Use the word in brackets.

1 You aren't old enough to drive. (young)

You are too young to drive.

2 I'm too short to reach that shelf. (tall)
3 You are too ill to go to school today. (well)
4 He isn't strong enough to lift that heavy box. (weak)
5 This T-shirt is too small for me. (big)
6 The tickets are too expensive. (cheap)
7 That theme park ride was boring. It was too slow! (fast)
8 We arrived too late to get the best seats in the cinema. (early)

much, many, a lot of

8 Complete the sentences with *much, many* or *a lot of.*

1 How *much* do you know about Scotland?
2 Do you know, for example, how .... castles there are?
3 They're planning to build a new library at our school. There's .... work to do.
4 Let's go somewhere else to eat. There are too .... people at this restaurant.
5 I can't buy that jacket. It costs too .... .
6 Wow! You've got so .... DVDs!
7 We don't need any more cola. There's .... cola left in the bottle.
8 How .... time have we got before the lesson starts?

Speaking   Describing a place

1 Put the conversation in the correct order.

1. What's your new house like?
.... Yes – there are a lot of flowers and trees in it.
.... Is it big?
.... Is the garden nice?
.... It's great!
.... Yes, it's bigger than our old house.

Mmm, when can I come and see it?
Come today, after school!

Permission

2 Complete the conversation with these words.

afraid	~~Can~~	can't	do	mind	OK

Paul [1] *Can* I go out with Alex tonight, Mum?
Mum No, you [2] .... . You've got to do your homework.
Paul Well, is it [3] .... if I go out after that?
Mum Yes, you can. But don't stay out too late.
Paul Er … Alex lives quite far away. Do you [4] .... if I stay over at Alex's house tonight?
Mum Yes, I [5] ....! You can't stay over on a school night.
Paul Well, can you give me a lift home?
Mum No, I'm [6] .... not, Paul. Perhaps you should stay at home after all.

Asking for help

3 Choose the correct option.

A Could you give me a [1] *hand / lend* with this heavy box, Steve?
B [2] *Sorry. / Sure.*
A Thanks. [3] *Would / Can* you mind [4] *carry / carrying* it to the station for me?
B Sorry, I [5] *don't / can't.* I'm meeting my friend in five minutes and we're going to watch a football match.
A Well, could you just carry it to the end of the road?
B [6] *No problem. / No sure.* You can get a taxi from there.

Vocabulary   Rooms and parts of the house

1 Complete the words for rooms and parts of the house.

1 There is an a *t t* i c at the top of the house.
2 Walk down the s _ _ _ rs to the c _ l _ a _ , below the house.
3 We haven't got a garden, but we've got a small p _ _ _ o.
4 We park the car in the g _ r _ _ e.
5 Our front d _ _ r is red.
6 The rooms have got very high c _ _ l _ _ gs.
7 My father works from home. He uses one room as his o _ f _ ce.

Review

Furniture and household objects

2 Match the words on the left (1–10) to the words on the right (a–j) to make furniture and household objects.

1	alarm	**a**	case
2	chest of	**b**	chair
3	ward	**c**	clock
4	arm	**d**	drawers
5	cur	**e**	ions
6	book	**f**	low
7	cush	**g**	robe
8	pil	**h**	ror
9	du	**i**	tains
10	mir	**j**	vet

Adjectives to describe pictures

3 Complete the sentences with these adjectives.

amusing	blurred	colourful	dull	fake
horrible	~~interesting~~	lovely	old-fashioned	silly

1 It doesn't look very *interesting* – it looks quite boring.
2 The photo isn't very clear. It's .... .
3 The colours are a bit .... . They're just grey and brown.
4 I love this picture – especially the .... red, orange and yellow flowers.
5 What a funny picture! It's very .... .
6 It isn't a modern picture. It's very .... .
7 Is it a real photo, or is it a .... ?
8 It isn't serious. It's just .... .
9 The picture of the park is .... – it's very pretty.
10 What an ugly place! It looks really .... .

Adjective + preposition

4 Complete the sentences with the correct preposition.

a If you get bored ¹ *with* listening to music on your MP3 player, try downloading radio podcasts instead. There are podcasts for all kinds of programmes. If you are interested ² .... plays, you can listen to stories or dramas, too. I get tired ³ .... the same old music so I sometimes listen to an online radio station. I'm keen ⁴ .... hip hop so my favourite one is called HipHop FM.

b We're going to a theme park this weekend! I'm really excited ⁵ .... that. I'm not afraid ⁶ .... fast and dangerous rides. I love them!

c I hope I do well in my exams. I want my parents to be proud ⁷ .... me. I don't want them to be angry ⁸ .... me.

Shopping nouns

5 Complete the sentences with these words.

bargains	~~cashpoint~~	coins
customers	note	sale
shop assistant	shopping basket	market stall

1 You can take money out of a machine called a *cashpoint*.
2 When a shop has a .... , things are cheaper and you can find lots of .... .
3 A .... works in a shop and serves the .... .
4 How many items have you got in your .... ?
5 I've got a ten euro .... and some fifty cent .... in my pocket.
6 He sells fruit and vegetables at the market. His .... is near the entrance.

Money verbs

6 Choose the correct option.

Brixton is a very popular market in London. People come there from all over the world to ¹ *buy / borrow* things. Most items aren't very expensive so you can usually find something you can ² *cost / afford*. Markets are often cheaper than high street shops so you can ³ *save / win* money by shopping there. But stallholders usually want you to pay ⁴ *in / by* cash. They don't usually have machines for ⁵ *credit / spend* cards. If you want to go to the market, I'll ⁶ *borrow / lend* you a big shopping bag. You'll need it for all your bargains!

Word list

Unit 1   Home Sweet Home

Rooms and parts of the house

attic	/ˈætɪk/
balcony	/ˈbælkəni/
ceiling	/ˈsiːlɪŋ/
cellar	/ˈselə/
drive	/draɪv/
fireplace	/ˈfaɪəpleɪs/
floor	/flɔː/
garage	/ˈɡærɪdʒ, -ɑːʒ/
hall	/hɔːl/
landing	/ˈlændɪŋ/
lawn	/lɔːn/
office	/ˈɒfəs/
patio	/ˈpætiəʊ/
roof	/ruːf/
stairs	/steəz/
wall	/wɔːl/

Furniture and household objects

alarm clock	/əˈlɑːm klɒk/
armchair	/ˈɑːmtʃeə/
blind	/blaɪnd/
bookcase	/ˈbʊk-keɪs/
chest of drawers	/ˌtʃest əv ˈdrɔːz/
curtains	/ˈkɜːtnz/
cushions	/ˈkʊʃənz/
duvet	/ˈduːveɪ/
mirror	/ˈmɪrə/
pillow	/ˈpɪləʊ/
rug	/rʌɡ/
vase	/vɑːz/
wardrobe	/ˈwɔːdrəʊb/

Unit 2   What's The Story?

Adjectives to describe pictures

amusing	/əˈmjuːzɪŋ/
blurred	/blɜːd/
colourful	/ˈkʌləfəl/
dark	/dɑːk/
dramatic	/drəˈmætɪk/
dull	/dʌl/
fake	/feɪk/
horrible	/ˈhɒrəbəl/
interesting	/ˈɪntrəstɪŋ/
lovely	/ˈlʌvli/
old-fashioned	/ˌəʊld ˈfæʃənd/
silly	/ˈsɪli/

Adjective + preposition

afraid of	/əˈfreɪd əv/
angry with	/ˈæŋɡri wɪð, wɪθ/
bad at	/ˈbæd ət/
bored with	/ˈbɔːd wɪð, wɪθ/
excited about	/ɪkˈsaɪtəd əˌbaʊt/
good at	/ˈɡʊd ət/
interested in	/ˈɪntrəstəd ɪn/
keen on	/ˈkiːn ɒn/
popular with	/ˈpɒpjələ wɪð, wɪθ/
proud of	/ˈpraʊd əv/
sorry for	/ˈsɒri fə, fɔː/
tired of	/ˈtaɪəd əv/

Unit 3   It's A Bargain!

Shopping nouns

bargain	/ˈbɑːɡən/
cashpoint	/ˈkæʃpɔɪnt/
change	/tʃeɪndʒ/
coin	/kɔɪn/
customer	/ˈkʌstəmə/
high street	/ˈhaɪ striːt/
market stall	/ˌmɑːkət ˈstɔːl/
note	/nəʊt/
price	/praɪs/
products	/ˈprɒdʌkts/
queue	/kjuː/
sale	/seɪl/
shop assistant	/ˈʃɒp əˌsɪstənt/
shopping basket	/ˈʃɒpɪŋ ˌbɑːskət/
stallholder	/ˈstɔːlˌhəʊldə/

Money verbs

afford	/əˈfɔːd/
borrow	/ˈbɒrəʊ/
buy	/baɪ/
cost	/kɒst/
earn	/ɜːn/
lend	/lend/
pay by credit card	/ˌpeɪ baɪ ˈkredɪt kɑːd/
pay in cash	/ˌpeɪ ɪn ˈkæʃ/
save	/seɪv/
sell	/sel/
spend	/spend/
win	/wɪn/

4 In The News

Grammar	Present perfect; Present perfect vs Past simple
Vocabulary	News and media; Adverbs of manner
Speaking	Doubt and disbelief
Writing	A profile

LOCAL SCHOOL IN NEWS

BREAKING NEWS

HOTTEST SUMMER EVER!

Vocabulary News and media

1 ◉ 2.1 Match the pictures (1–4) to three or four of these words and complete the table. Then listen, check and repeat.

blog	current affairs programme
headline	international news
interview	journalist
local news	national news
news flash	newspaper
news presenter	news website
podcast	report (v, n)

> **Word list** page 77   **Workbook** page 107

2 Complete the sentences with the words in Exercise 1.

1 The *headlines* in today's *newspapers* are all about the football match.
2 I'd love to be a .... on TV or for a newspaper and .... important people.
3 I want to start a .... on the internet so I can write about my holidays.
4 I often read *Teen News* on my computer. It's a .... for teenagers.
5 I don't usually download .... , but this one is interesting. It's an interview with Justin Bieber.
6 My uncle's a .... . He reads the news on a .... .

3 In pairs, ask and answer.

1 Do you prefer to read the news in a newspaper or online?
2 What was the last news story you read about?
3 Can you name any news presenters?
4 Do you prefer local news or international news?

NEWSSPOTtravel
BLOGSPOT PODSPOT
DESTINATION NEW YORK
by Sam Welling
▶ Jamie Tan: talks to tourists in Paris
▶ Tommy Jo:

	1	2	3	4
news presenter	.....	.....	.....
.....	.....	.....	.....
.....	.....	.....	.....
.....	.....		

I prefer reading a newspaper. What about you?

I like reading news online – it's quicker!

Brain Trainer Unit 4
Activity 2 Go to page 114

Reading

1 You are going to read a survey about teens and the news. Look at the photo and answer the questions.

   1 What is the girl doing?
   2 What do you think she is reading about?
   3 Do your family or friends read a print newspaper?

2 Can you predict the results of the survey? Complete the sentences with these numbers.

  ~~85~~   51   35   31   16   69

   85 % of teenagers watch news flashes about important events.
   .... % of teenagers watch the news on TV.
   .... % log on to news websites.
   .... % read the news every day.
   .... % watch current affairs programmes.
   .... % could live without newspapers.

3 Read the survey quickly and check your answers to Exercise 2.

4 🔊 2.2   Read the survey again. Answer the questions.

   1 What type of news are teens interested in?
     National news.
   2 How many teens think newspapers are important?
   3 How did Jake find out about the tsunami in Japan?
   4 Why does he like news websites?
   5 Why doesn't Lily read the news every day?
   6 Where does she usually read a newspaper?
   7 Which stories does she read?

5 **What about you?** In pairs, ask and answer the four questions in the survey.

Survey: Teens and the media

In last month's issue of *Teen News* we asked you to email us your answers to the following questions:

- Have you read or heard today's news headlines?
- Where do you usually get your news from?
- Do you read or listen to the news every day?
- What news are you interested in?

Here are the results!
Most of you (sixty-nine percent) prefer watching the news on TV and thirty-five percent regularly log on to news websites. Thirty-one percent of you read or listen to the news every day, but only sixteen percent like watching current affairs programmes. You're more interested in national news than international news, but nearly eighty-five percent of our readers watch news flashes about important events in the world.

So, is there any room for newspapers in today's world? Twenty-three percent of you said 'yes', but more than half (fifty-one percent) said you could live without them. Jake and Lily explain their views:

Jake Moreno (16)
I've never bought a newspaper. I usually find out about the news through a social networking site. That's how I heard about the tsunami in Japan. One of my friends added a link to a news flash. News websites are good, too because you can listen to podcasts and watch videos.

Lily Sheldon (15)
I sometimes look at news websites, but I haven't had time this week (too much homework!). I usually read a newspaper on the school bus. I follow the local news and I also read the sports reports.

Grammar   Present perfect

Affirmative

I/You/We/They have ('ve) read the news.
He/She/It has ('s) read the news.

Negative

I/You/We/They have not (haven't) read the news.
He/She/It has not (hasn't) read the news.

Questions and short answers

Have I/you/we/they heard the news?
Yes, I/you/we/they have. / No, I/you/we/they haven't.

Has he/she/it heard the news?
Yes, he/she/it has. / No, he/she/it hasn't.

Watch Out!

Have you ever bought a newspaper?
He has never bought a newspaper.

Grammar reference Workbook page 92

**1   Study the grammar table and Watch Out!
Complete the rules with these words.**

an unspecified past time	ever	have/has	never

1 We use the Present perfect to talk about an experience that happened at .... .
2 We make the Present perfect with .... and the Past participle.
3 We use .... to ask about experiences.
4 We use .... to talk about experiences we haven't had.

2   Complete the sentences with the Present perfect form of these verbs.

buy	invite	~~not buy~~	not finish
not go	not hear	see	write

1 Sorry – I *haven't bought* a newspaper. I haven't had time!
2 My sister is a journalist. She .... lots of articles.
3 A .... she .... you to her party?
  B No, she hasn't!
4 I can't go out tonight. I .... my homework.
5 He .... a new mobile phone – it's black and yellow!
6 We .... that horror film before – it was really scary.
7 They .... to the beach today. It's too cold!
8 I .... the football results. Did we win?

3))) 2.3   Complete the conversation. Then listen and check.

Girl [1] *Have* you *seen* (see) the new school website?
Boy No, I [2] ..... . Is it good?
Girl It's great! It's got school news, film reviews and jokes on it.
Boy What about football? [3] ... the sports teacher .... (write) about the school team match?
Girl No, he [4] .... . Why don't you write about it?
Boy I don't know how to write a report. [5] .... you .... (ever/do) something like that?
Girl Yes, I [6] ..... . I [7] .... (write) about school uniforms for the school newspaper before and I [8] .... (interview) some teachers. You should interview the head teacher.
Boy No way! I [9] .... (not interview) anyone before!
Girl Well, listen to mine first. They [10] .... (put) a podcast of my interviews on the website.

4   Complete the questions and answers.

1 A *Have you ever been* (you/ever/be) to the USA?
  B Yes, I have.
2 A .... (you/ever/meet) a famous person?
  B No, I .... (never/meet) a famous person.
3 A .... (you/ever/play) basketball?
  B Yes, I .... .
4 A .... (he/ever/write) a blog?
  B No, he .... (never/write) a blog.
5 A .... (she/ever/be) late for school?
  B Yes, she .... !
6 A .... (you/ever/wear) a long dress?
  B No, I .... (never/wear) a long dress.
7 A .... (they/ever/buy) a computer game?
  B Yes, they .... .

5   What about you? In pairs, ask and answer.

Have you ever …

• go to a rock concert?
• wear red trainers?
• try skateboarding?
• see a horror film?
• had a pet?
• write a poem?
• be on TV?
• stand on your head?

Have you ever been to a rock concert?

Yes, I have. It was fantastic!

Vocabulary   Adverbs of manner

1 🔊 **2.4** **Look at these words. Check the meaning in a dictionary. Listen and repeat.**

angrily	badly	carefully	carelessly	early
fast	happily	hard	late	loudly
patiently	quietly	sadly	slowly	~~well~~

Word list page 77   **Workbook** page 107

2 **Complete the sentences with the words in Exercise 1.**

1 He's a good journalist. He writes very *well*.
2 She's a hard worker. She works very .... .
3 It was a sad news story. He read it .... .
4 They were late for the party. They arrived .... .
5 He's very quiet. He speaks .... , too.
6 The politician was angry. He answered the questions .... .
7 They're slow readers. They read .... .
8 He's so careless. He does things .... .

3 **Choose the correct options to complete the text.**

How to be a news presenter

TV news presenters work very ¹ *hard / badly*. Have you ever got up at 5 a.m. in the morning? Well, I get up very ² *early / late* every day. When I get to the TV studio there's a lot of information to read. I read it ³ *slowly / fast* so I know the main stories. I read it again later to get more detail. Then a hairdresser does my hair and I choose my clothes ⁴ *carefully / carelessly*. You can't wear black, white or red – cameras have problems with these colours! I'm always ready early but I wait ⁵ *angrily / patiently* for the show to start, then I smile ⁶ *sadly / happily* and read the news headlines. I speak clearly (but not too ⁷ *quietly / loudly*) so people can understand what I say. It's an interesting job and I do it ⁸ *badly / well*!

4 **Correct the sentences. Use these words.**

badly	carefully	early	fast
happily	~~loudly~~	patiently	

1 The class sang **quietly**. It was really noisy. *loudly*
2 Jed spent a long time taking the photo. He did it very **carelessly**.
3 Kylie smiled **sadly** when she won first prize.
4 We ran very **slowly**. We were late for school!
5 Kurt did **well** in his exams. He didn't get good grades.
6 The teacher explained the homework **angrily**. He wanted everyone to understand.
7 The train arrived **late** so we got to the show on time.

5 **What about you? In pairs, ask and answer.**

1 Do you work slowly or fast?
2 Do you get to school early or late?
3 Do you work hard in class?
4 Do you usually play your music loudly or quietly?
5 Do you usually do well or badly in school exams?

Pronunciation   /æ/ and /ɑː/

6a 🔊 **2.5** **Listen and repeat.**

/æ/	/ɑː/
flash	dark
happily	far
have	hard

b 🔊 **2.6** **Listen. Copy the table and put these words in the correct column.**

~~album~~	angrily	badly	~~basket~~	card
class	hat	park	party	sadly

/æ/	/ɑː/
album	*basket*

c 🔊 **2.7** **Listen, check and repeat.**

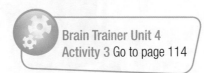

Brain Trainer Unit 4
Activity 3 Go to page 114

Chatroom Doubt and disbelief

Speaking and Listening

1 **Look at the photo. Answer the questions.**

1 Where are the teenagers?
2 What are they doing?
3 What do you think has happened?

2 🔊 2.8 **Listen and read the conversation. Check your answers.**

3 🔊 2.8 **Listen and read again. Answer the questions.**

1 What escaped from the zoo?
   A snake.
2 Where did they find it?
3 Who found it?
4 What did she think it was?
5 What was probably terrified?
6 Who isn't scared of snakes?

4 **Act out the conversation in groups of four.**

Tom	Hey, have you heard the story about the snake?
Ash	What snake?
Tom	The snake from the zoo. It escaped last week. Well, they've found it.
Ash	Have they? Where?
Tom	In a shop in town.
Ash	No, really?
Tom	Yes, listen to this: 'Carrie James, a local teenager, found the snake when she was shopping in Trend clothes shop yesterday.'
Ella	I don't believe it! I shop there all the time.
Tom	'I thought it was a scarf,' said Carrie, 'but when I touched it, it moved away quickly.'
Ash	That's ridiculous!
Tom	It gets better. 'I've never touched a snake before,' said Carrie. 'I'm glad I didn't try it on!'
Ella	Ugh! Imagine that!
Ruby	Poor snake! It was probably terrified.
Ella	Poor snake? You're joking!
Ruby	No, I'm not. I really like snakes.

Say it in your language …
It gets better.
Imagine that!

5 Look back at the conversation. Who says what?

1 No, really? *Ash*
2 I don't believe it!
3 That's ridiculous!
4 You're joking!

6 Read the phrases for expressing doubt and disbelief.

Expressing doubt and disbelief
No, really?
I don't believe it.
That's strange.
That's impossible.
You're joking!
That's ridiculous!

7 🔊 **2.9** **Listen to the conversations. Act out the conversations in pairs.**

Ruby I met [1] Justin Bieber in LA last week.
Tom I don't believe it.
Ruby But it's true!

Ella [2] Our school was on TV yesterday.
Ruby That's impossible!
Ella No, it isn't. Have a look at [3] the news website.

Tom I've put [4] a video of my dog online.
Ash You're joking!
Tom No, I'm not. Here it is.

8 Work in pairs. Replace the words in purple in Exercise 7. Use these words and/or your own ideas. Act out the conversations.

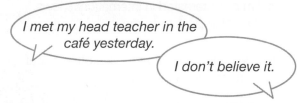

I met my head teacher in the café yesterday.

I don't believe it.

1 Lady Gaga in London / Daniel Craig in Hollywood / David Beckham in Madrid

2 my best friend / my dad / my brother

3 the local news / my blog

4 a photo of my party / a video of my cat / a picture of me in my Superman costume

Grammar Present perfect vs Past simple

Present perfect	Past simple
A snake has escaped from the zoo.	A snake escaped from the zoo last week.
I've never touched a snake before.	She didn't touch the snake.
Have they found the snake?	A teenager found the snake in a shop yesterday.

▷ **Grammar reference** Workbook page 92

1 Study the grammar table. Choose the correct options to complete the rules.

1 We use the *Past simple / Present perfect* to talk about something that happened at an unspecified time in the past.
2 We use the *Past simple / Present perfect* to talk about something that happened at a specific time in the past.

2 Complete the sentences with the Past simple or Present perfect form of the verbs.

1 finish
a I've *finished* my homework. Can I watch TV?
b I *finished* my homework half an hour ago.

2 eat
a Who .... the pizza? It's all gone!
b We .... a really nice pizza last night.

3 not go
a We .... on holiday – we've been on a school trip.
b We .... on holiday last year.

4 lose
a I .... my glasses at the cinema last weekend.
b I .... my glasses. I can't see anything!

3 Make conversations.

A you ever / meet a famous person?
Have you ever met a famous person?
B Yes, I have.
A Really? Who / you / meet?
B I / meet Keira Knightley last year.
A you / ever be / to a skatepark?
B Yes, I have.
A When / you / go?
B I / go / to one last week.

Reading

1 **Look at the photo. Answer the questions.**

1 What do you think the woman's job is?

2 How would you describe her work?

- dangerous
- boring
- easy
- safe
- interesting
- difficult

Profile: Christiane Amanpour

Christiane Amanpour is small with dark hair. She looks like an ordinary person, but she is one of the world's most famous journalists.

Christiane was born in England in 1958 and went to school
5 there and in Iran. She studied journalism in America and when she finished university, she got a job as an assistant with CNN. 'I arrived at CNN with a suitcase, my bicycle and 100 dollars,' she says. It was a difficult introduction to journalism, but Christiane worked hard and she soon
10 became a foreign correspondent.
Life as a foreign correspondent is busy and often dangerous. They fly to different countries and report on international news there. Their reports appear on news websites, in newspapers and on TV and thousands,
15 sometimes millions, of people see them.
Christiane has been all over the world and reported on

many different stories. Some of them are the biggest stories of the twentieth century. She has reported on wars and natural disasters and she has also interviewed world
20 leaders and politicians. She has often been in danger, but luckily she has never had an injury. Christiane won the Courage in Journalism Award in 1994 for her war reports, but she is modest about it. 'It's our job to go to these places and bring back stories, just as a window on the
25 world,' she says.
Today, Christiane is a news presenter on a current affairs programme called *This Week*. She interviews people in a TV studio, so she doesn't travel much, but she still tells people what is happening in the world. 'I believe that good
30 journalism, good television, can make our world a better place,' she says.

Key Words

foreign correspondent	wars
natural disasters	world leaders
politicians	modest

2 **Read the magazine article and check your answers to Exercise 1.**

3 (( )) 2.10 **Read the article again. Answer the questions.**

1 Why is Christiane Amanpour special?

She is one of the world's most famous journalists.

2 Where did she study journalism?

3 What was her first job?

4 What do foreign correspondents do?

5 What kind of stories has Christiane reported on?

6 Why did she win the Courage in Journalism Award?

7 What does Christiane do at the moment?

4 **What do these words refer to?**

1 there (line 5) – *in England*

2 she (line 9)

3 them (line 15)

4 them (line 17)

5 it (line 23)

Listening

1 **Look at these opinions about the news. Which do you agree with?**

a I'm not interested in international news. It's not important to me.

b The news is usually bad. It's often about wars or natural disasters.

c It's good to know what is happening in the world.

(( )) 2.11 **Listening Bank Unit 4** page 118

2 **Think about a story in the news this week. Answer the questions.**

1 Is it national, international or local news?

2 Where did you see it? In a newspaper, on a news website, on TV?

3 What is the story about?

Writing   A profile

1   Read the Writing File.

2   Read the profile. Find and correct six errors.

• two punctuation
• two spelling
• two grammar

1 *canterbury – Canterbury*

👤 Profile: Orlando Bloom

Orlando Bloom is a great actor and is often in the newspapers, but I admire him because of his work for UNICEF *.

Orlando was born in 1977 in a town called canterbury. He has gone to school there with his sister, Samantha. Reading and riting weren't easy for Orlando, but he always wanted to be an actor After school, he studied drama in London, then he got the part of Legolas in *The Lord of the Rings*. Today, Orlando was very famous, but he's used his fame to help other people. He has visited schools and villages in Nepal and has helped to support clean water and education progammes there. Orlando Bloom is not just a pretty face, he cares about people and the world around him. That's why I admire him.

* UNICEF is the United Nations children's charity

3   Look at these sentences about the actor, Orlando Bloom. Find and correct the errors.
(S = spelling, G = grammar, P = punctuation)

1 Orlando Bloom is ofen in the newspapers. (S) *often*
2 His most exiting film is *Pirates of the Caribbean*. (S)
3 When he was 15, he has had a tattoo. (G)
4 Orlando broke his nose while he is playing rugby. (G)
5 He has a dog called sidi. (P)
6 Is he working in Hollywood at the moment. (P)

4   Read the profile again. Answer the questions.

1 Who did Orlando go to school with?
   His sister Samantha
2 What did Orlando always want to be?
3 Where did he study drama?
4 What part did he play in *The Lord of the Rings*?
5 How has he helped other people?
6 Why does the writer admire Orlando Bloom?

5   Think about a famous person in the news who you admire and find out about them. Answer these questions. Make notes.

1 Why is he/she famous?
2 Why do you admire him/her?
3 When was he/she born?
4 Has he/she got brothers and sisters?
5 Where did he/she go to school?
6 What does he/she do today?

6   Write a profile of the person you chose in Exercise 5. Use 'My famous person' and your notes from Exercise 5.

My famous person

Paragraph 1
Introduction and why you admire him/her
.... (name) *is a great* .... (job). *I admire him/her because of his/her* ..... .

Paragraph 2
Early life, education and career
.... *was born in* .... (when?) *in* .... (where?). *After school, he/she* ... (what did he/she do?)

Paragraph 3
What he/she has done recently and why you admire him/her
Today .... (name) *is* .... (describe him/her). *He/She has* ... (what has he/she done recently).

Remember!
• Use the vocabulary from this and earlier units where possible.
• Check your grammar, spelling and punctuation.

Refresh Your Memory!

Grammar Review

1 Complete the text about a famous reporter. Use the Present perfect form of the verbs.

Clark Kent works for the *Daily Planet*. He's tired because he ¹ *'s had* (have) a busy day. What ² .... he .... (do)? Well, he ³ .... (meet) the Mayor of Metropolis and he ⁴ .... (write) a report for the newspaper. He ⁵ .... (work) with his friend, Lois, on a big story. They ⁶ .... (not finish) it because they ⁷ .... (not interview) Lex Luther. Clark ⁸ .... (not see) Lex today, but he ⁹ .... (fly) around the city and helped people. Clark Kent has two jobs. ¹⁰ .... you .... (ever/hear) of Superman?

2 Make sentences and questions.

1 you / ever / read / a newspaper on the bus?

Have you ever read a newspaper on the bus?

2 I / never / play / ice hockey
3 they / ever / watch / a video online?
4 He / never / act / in a film
5 she / ever / interview / a pop star?
6 We / never / try / playing rugby
7 you / ever / hear / an Arctic Monkeys' song?

3 Choose the correct options.

1 Some teenagers *have never bought / never bought* a newspaper.
2 Pete *has read / read* an interesting blog about computer games last night.
3 There *has been / was* a news flash about a tsunami this morning.
4 She *has never eaten / didn't eat* at a pizzeria. She doesn't like pizzas.
5 We *haven't seen / didn't see* the football match last weekend.
6 I *have never had / didn't have* my own computer, but I want one for my birthday.

Vocabulary Review

4 Read the definitions and complete the words.

1 You can listen to this on your MP3 player. p<u>o</u>dca<u>s</u>t
2 You can see this person on TV. n_ws pr_s_nt_r
3 This person often writes for a newspaper. j_ _rn_l_st
4 The most important news stories are the h_ _dl_n_s.
5 A story in a newspaper is called a r_p_rt.
6 Important new stories usually appear in a n_wsfl_sh on TV.
7 People use this to write about their everyday lives. bl_g
8 On a computer, we can read the news on a n_ws w_bs_t_ .
9 A TV programme about important stories in the news. c_rr_nt _ff_ _rs pr_gr_mm_

5 Complete the sentences with the correct adverb form of the adjective in brackets.

1 The actress is smiling *happily* (happy) in the photo.
2 My brother is playing his music very .... (loud).
3 Peter always does his homework very .... (careful).
4 I play tennis really .... (bad).
5 The reporter waited .... (patient) for the interview to begin.
6 The bus doesn't go very .... (fast), but it's cheaper than the train.

Speaking Review

6 🔊 2.12 Complete the conversation with these words. Then listen and check.

happen	headlines	~~heard~~	impossible	joking

Girl Have you ¹ *heard* the news? An elephant has escaped from the zoo.
Boy That's ² .... !
Girl No, it isn't. Look at the ³ .... . I'm not ⁴ .... .
Boy Wow! It <u>is</u> true. That's ridiculous!
Girl I know, but how did it ⁵ .... ?

Dictation

7 🔊 2.13 Listen and write in your notebook.

✓ My assessment profile: Workbook page 130

Real World Profiles

Amy Grey's Profile

Age:
15 years old

Home country:
Canada

My favourite things …

fashion, writing (check out my fashion blog), photography, reading magazines

Reading

1 Read Amy's profile. Are the sentences true (T) or false (F)?

1 Amy is from the USA. *F*
2 She likes taking photos.
3 She has a news website.
4 She goes to fashion shows in London.

2 🔊 **2.14** Read the article. Answer the questions.

1 How old was Amy when she started her blog?
She was 11.
2 Who takes photos for Amy's blog?
3 Why is Toronto a good city for Amy to write her blog about?
4 How many people read Amy's blog?
5 Why doesn't Amy buy designer clothes?
6 How does Amy suggest her readers save money on clothes?

Amy Grey: Fashion Blogger

Amy Grey was born in 1998. She has three older brothers and lives with her parents in Toronto, Canada. When she was a  child, Amy became interested in fashion and photography. She loved to look at her mum's fashion magazines and started to notice the different styles and trends on the streets of Toronto. Then, when she was just 11 years old, Amy decided to write about them. With a little help from her parents, she started a fashion blog called Toronto Streetside.

Amy's blog is an online diary, with opinions about street fashion as well as general fashion news. All of the photography is by Amy herself and is very professional, with entertaining commentary and sometimes quotes from people in the pictures. 'I love watching people in parks or cafés, on the subway or at tram stops. There's so much style in this city,' explains Amy. The changing climate in Toronto (sub-zero in winter and often 30°C in summer) means that people wear a lot of different clothing, too. 'It's exciting when I spot an interesting "look",' she adds. 'It may be someone with the latest brand combined with something retro, or something of sentimental value. They could be a bicycle courier, a market stall trader, a cab driver, anyone really. And I always talk to the people I photograph - it's fascinating to hear the story behind the outfit.'

Today, six years after she started her blog, Amy has more than 30,000 readers. Fashion magazines like *Vogue* and *Elle* often publish her photos and opinions and designers invite her to fashion shows in Canada and the USA. 'It's great going to the shows,' she says. 'Although I can't afford the clothes!' Does that worry her at all? 'Not really,' she says. 'It's surprising what you can find in sales and second-hand shops. You don't need to spend a lot of money to be creative and look good.'

Key Words

| styles | trends | a 'look' |
| latest | brand | retro |

Class discussion

1 Do you read any blogs on the internet? What are they about?
2 Do you know any famous fashion designers from your country?
3 What type of clothes do you buy? Do you like designer clothes or do you look for bargains like Amy?

5 Happy Holidays

Grammar	Present perfect + *for* and *since*; *How long?*; Present perfect with *just*
Vocabulary	Holidays; Meanings of *get*
Speaking	Asking for information
Writing	A travel guide

Vocabulary Holidays

1 🔊 2.15 **Match the pictures (1–14) to these activities. Then listen, check and repeat.**

book a holiday *1*	buy souvenirs	check into a hotel
eat out	get a tan	get lost
go abroad	go camping	lose your luggage
pack your bag	put up a tent	see the sights
stay in a hotel	write a travel blog	

Word list page 77   **Workbook** page 108

2 Match the sentences to the activities in Exercise 1.

1 OK, we've got flights and paid for the villa – I think that's everything. *book a holiday*
2 All the other bags have gone, but mine wasn't there!
3 This pink T-shirt is great. It says 'I love New York'.
4 I've almost finished, but the bag is really heavy!
5 I want to see the famous cathedral by Gaudi.
6 My best friend is flying to Australia next week.
7 Shall we go to the restaurant by the beach tonight?
8 I'm not sure how to get back to the hotel!

3 Match the verbs (1–6) to the nouns (a–f) to make activities from Exercise 1.

1 stay   a into a hotel
2 write   b a tan
3 go   c a tent
4 check   d a travel blog
5 get   e in a hotel
6 put up   f camping

4 What about you? **In pairs, ask and answer.**

1 Where do you usually stay when you go on holiday?
2 What do you enjoy doing? Do you like getting a tan or seeing the sights?
3 Have you ever written a travel blog?

I usually stay in a hotel.

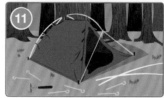

Brain Trainer Unit 5
Activity 2 Go to page 114

Reading

1 Look at the photos from Shannon and Gemma's holiday. Answer the questions.

   1 What type of holiday is it?
   2 Where do you think they are staying?
   3 What do you think they do every day?

2 Read the magazine article quickly and check your answers to Exercise 1. Which activity in the photos haven't Shannon and Gemma done?

3 🔊 2.16 Read the article again. Answer the questions.

   Who …
   1 likes staying in hotels? *Shannon*
   2 likes doing different activities?
   3 has never booked a holiday before?
   4 has never stayed in a tent before?
   5 gets bored easily?
   6 sometimes listens to music?
   7 usually reads books on holiday?
   8 has enjoyed the holiday?

4 **What about you?** **In pairs ask and answer.**

   1 What do your parents like to do on holiday? Do you like the same things or different things?
   2 What are the advantages of a family holiday? Are there any disadvantages?

> **Advantages**
> Stay in a nice hotel.
> Parents pay for everything.
>
> **Disadvantages**
> Can't stay up late.
> Difficult to meet other teenagers.

BEHIND THE CAMERA

People have different ideas about what makes a good holiday, especially parents and their children. In a new TV show *You choose!*, kids decide on the family holiday, with some funny results! This week, 16-year-old Gemma Roberts packs the bags and books the holiday destination. Mum, Shannon, gets a big surprise. We asked them about their experiences.

"I think Mum liked canoeing ..."

Gemma's story

Mum has always chosen our holidays since I was small. We usually stay in hotels and Mum just likes getting a tan or she reads books all day. I don't mind swimming or listening to my MP3 player, but I like adventure too, so I chose a holiday in the Lake District. No hotels, no swimming pools, just a tent in a field (Mum has never put up a tent before). How long have we been here? Mum says 'forever!', but actually we've been here for five days. We've tried mountain biking, rock climbing and canoeing since the weekend. Mum was scared on the rock climb, but I think she liked canoeing ...

Shannon's story

I was worried when Gemma chose the holiday. I like to relax and read when I'm away, but Gemma is quite active. She often gets bored. It hasn't been a great holiday because I haven't read a book since Saturday. In fact I haven't read anything for a whole week, but I've had some time to talk to Gemma. That's been the best part, really. We're both too busy to talk at home!

Grammar Present perfect + *for* and *since*; *How long*?

> How long have we been here?
> We've been here for five days/a week/a month.

> I haven't read a book since Saturday.

> She's lived in France since 2010.

> Grammar reference Workbook page 94

1 Study the grammar table. Choose the correct options to complete the rules.

> **1** We use *for / since* with a period of time.
> **2** We use *for / since* with a point in time.

2 Copy the table and put these words and phrases in the correct column.

~~a long time~~	a week	~~August~~	four years
five o'clock	I was fifteen	last week	ten minutes
the weekend	Tuesday	two days	yesterday

for	since
a long time	*August*

3 Make sentences with the Present perfect. Add *for* or *since* to each sentence.

1 They / not go / abroad / years

They haven't gone abroad for years.

2 You / be on my games console / hours!
3 He / not watch TV / last weekend
4 We / stay in the same hotel / two weeks
5 I / not write my travel blog / a long time
6 We / eat local food / we arrived
7 They / not see their friends / Friday

4 Complete the text about an unusual holiday. Use the verbs or choose *for* or *since*.

Jilly Daniels ¹ *has had* (have) a new bike ² *for / since* Christmas. When she got her bike, she went on a cycling holiday. She ³ .... (be) on her holiday ⁴ *for / since* three months now and she ⁵ .... (travel) thousands of kilometres. She ⁶ .... (visit) six different countries and she ⁷ .... (be) in Portugal ⁸ *for / since* Thursday. However, she ⁹ .... (not stay) in a hotel or put up a tent ¹⁰ *for / since* December. Why? Because Jilly's bike ¹¹ .... (not leave) her house! 'It's a virtual holiday on an exercise bike,' explains Jilly. 'I cycle 20 kilometres at home every day. I follow a map, then I read about the place I'm 'visiting' on the internet. I haven't got a tan and I ¹² .... (not buy) any souvenirs,' she says, 'but I'm enjoying it!'

5 Make questions and answers about Exercise 4.

1 How long / Jilly / had a new bike?

How long has Jilly had a new bike? Since Christmas.

2 How long / she / be on holiday?
3 How long / she / be in Portugal?
4 How many kilometres / she / travel?
5 How many countries / she visit?
6 How many souvenirs / she / buy?

Pronunciation /aɪ/ vs /ɪ/

6a))) 2.17 Listen and repeat.

| active | arrive | bike | give | I've | like |
| live | mobile | miss | since | time | visit |

b Copy the table and put the words in Exercise 6a in the correct column.

/aɪ/	/ɪ/
arrive	*active*

c))) 2.18 Listen, check and repeat.

---

7 What about you? In pairs, ask and answer.
1 How long have you lived in your town?
2 How long have you had a mobile phone?
3 How long have you known your best friend?

> How long have you lived in your town?

> I've lived here for ten years.

Vocabulary   Meanings of *get*

1 Match the pictures (1–6) to the different meanings of the verb *get* (a–f).

   a It was dark when we got to the campsite. = arrive

   b Damian got a key ring and a baseball cap from the souvenir shop. = buy *1*

   c We got their postcard after they arrived back from their holiday. = receive

   d Can you get the suntan lotion from the hotel room? = fetch

   e It was getting cold on the beach so we went home. = become

   f He got on the bus and bought a ticket. = walk/move

> **Word list** page 77   **Workbook** page 108

LETTERS

2 Read the sentences. Replace *get* with one of these verbs in the correct form.

~~arrive~~	become	buy	fetch	receive	walk

   1 Hurry up! We won't get to school on time!
   Hurry up! We won't arrive at school on time.

   2 I think adventure holidays are getting more dangerous.

   3 When you book a flight online, you get the tickets in an email.

   4 She got a lot of new clothes for her holiday.

   5 Can you get the guidebook? I left it in my bag.

   6 Someone checked our passports before we got onto the plane.

3 What would you say in these situations? Make a question or a sentence with *get*.

   1 You like your friend's new bag. You want to know where she bought it.
   Where did you get your bag?

   2 You sent your friend a text message. You want to know if he received it.
   Did you .... ?

   3 You see your friends at a party. You ask them what time they arrived.
   When .... ?

   4 You are at a train station with a friend. Your train has just arrived.
   Come on. Let's .... .

   5 Your mother has left her jacket upstairs. You offer to fetch it for her.
   Don't worry. I'll .... .

4 **What about you?** In pairs, ask and answer.

   1 How many text messages do you get a day?

   2 What time do you usually get to school?

   3 What things can you do to get healthy?

   4 How often do you get on a bus to go to school?

> *How many text messages do you get a day?*
>
> *I get about twenty text messages a day.*

Brain Trainer Unit 5
Activity 3 Go to page 115

Chatroom Asking for information

Speaking and Listening

1 **Look at the photo. Answer the questions.**

1 Where do you think they have been?
2 What are they doing?
3 What do you think Tom's dad is asking?

2 🔊 2.19 **Listen and read the conversation. Check your answers.**

3 🔊 2.19 **Listen and read again. Answer the questions.**

1 Who liked the souvenir shops? *Tom*
2 What does Ash want to do?
3 Where does Tom want to go next?
4 How does the girl help them?
5 How can they get there?
6 What does Ash want to know?

4 **Act out the conversation in groups of four.**

Mr Green	What did you think of Brighton Pier, boys?
Tom	Great! I really liked the souvenir shops.
Ash	The cafés were nice, too. Can we have lunch soon?
Tom	You've just had an ice cream, Ash! Let's go and see Brighton Pavilion first.
Ash	Is it far?
Mr Green	Let's ask someone. Excuse me. Can you help us? We want to get to Brighton Pavilion.
Girl	Sure. Let me show you on the map. You're here … and Brighton Pavilion is there. You can't miss it.
Mr Green	How can we get there?
Girl	Well, you've just missed the bus, but it's only ten minutes on foot.
Ash	Is there a good place to eat there?
Girl	Oh yes! There's a really good restaurant there. The menu has just changed and the food's delicious.
Ash	Thank goodness. I'm starving!

Say it in your language …
Thank goodness.
I'm starving!

5 **Look back at the conversation. Who says what?**

1 Is it far? *Ash*
2 Excuse me. Can you help us?
3 How can we get there?
4 Is there a good place to eat there?

6 **Read the phrases for asking for information.**

Asking for information
Excuse me. Can you help us/me?
Where's a good place to …?
Is there a good place to … there?
How can we/I get there?
Is it far?
How long does it take to get to …?

7))) 2.20 **Listen to the conversations. What information do the people ask for? Act out the conversations in pairs.**

Ash   Excuse me. Can you help us? Where's a good place to ¹ eat out?
Girl   There's a ² pizzeria by the beach.
Ash   Thanks. That's great.

Tom   Excuse me. Can you help me?
Girl   Sure.
Tom   Where's a good place to ¹ buy souvenirs?
Girl   There's a ² great shop in the Brighton Pavilion.
Tom   Is it far?
Girl   ³ No, it's only five minutes on foot.

8 **Work in pairs. Replace the words in purple in Exercise 7. Use these words and/or your own ideas. Act out the conversations.**

> *Excuse me. Can you help us? Where's a good place to buy a map?*

> *There's a newsagent's by the station.*

1 buy clothes / have a drink / go swimming

2 good shop on the high street / café by the pier / swimming pool near the park

3 No, it's about five minutes by bus. / Yes, it's about twenty minutes on foot. / No, it's just over there.

Grammar   Present perfect with *just*

You've just had an ice cream.
You've just missed the bus.
The menu has just changed.

> **Grammar reference** Workbook page 94

1 **Study the grammar table. Choose the correct option to complete the rule.**

> The Present perfect with *just* describes an action that happened *a short time ago / a long time ago*.

2 **Make sentences with *just*.**
1 He / get some fish and chips
   He's just got some fish and chips.
2 I / get a postcard from my friend
3 She / be for a swim
4 We / pack our bags
5 He / buy some souvenirs
6 I / find the guidebook
7 They / check into their hotel

3 **In pairs, say what has just happened. Use the ideas below.**

book a holiday	his brother/tell a joke
leave the house	lose their luggage
put up a tent	start homework
their team/win a match	

1 He's excited.
2 They're worried.
3 We're tired.
4 He's laughing.
5 She isn't at home.
6 They're happy.
7 You're bored.

> *Why is he excited?*

> *He's just booked a holiday.*

Reading

1 Look at the photos of these tourist attractions. Which would you like to visit? Why?

Strange Tourist Attractions

This week in *Holiday Horizons* you can read about tourist attractions with a difference.

Bubblegum Alley, San Luis Obispo, USA
In 1950, this was just a normal passage between buildings. Then, students from two local schools started to leave their bubblegum on its walls. They wrote messages with the gum and made pictures. Some people loved the bubblegum in the alley, but others hated it and local shopkeepers cleaned it a few times. But the students and their bubblegum always came back. Today the alley is called Bubblegum Alley and it is still full of gum. Students leave most of it, but tourists and artists leave gum, too. Artist Matthew Hoffman has recently made a big picture of a man blowing a bubble! 'It's fantastic!' says one visitor. 'Disgusting!' says another. What do you think?

Upside Down House, Szymbark, Poland
Daniel Czapiewski built this house in 2007 and thousands of tourists have visited it since then. He built it because he thinks many things in the world are wrong – upside down – and his house is a symbol of this.

You usually enter a house through the door, but to get into the Upside Down House, you climb through a window. When you are inside, you walk along the ceiling, go under a table and look up at a bed. In the bathroom, there's a toilet on the ceiling and in the living room there's an upside down TV.

Inside the house, there's an art exhibition. It's called 'Let's save this world' and the pictures show different world problems. Czapiewski wants people to think about these things. 'I've just visited the house and I like its message,' said one tourist, 'but it made me feel dizzy!'

Key Words

tourist attractions   passage
bubblegum   shopkeepers
blowing a bubble   upside down
dizzy

2 🔊 **2.21** Read the magazine article. Match the statements with the attractions.

A = Bubblegum Alley
B = Upside Down House

1 Some people don't like it. *A*
2 Furniture is in the wrong place.
3 It's popular with students.
4 It has something important to say.
5 You can walk along it.
6 You feel confused inside.
7 You can see serious pictures there.
8 You can see a funny picture there.

3 Read the article again. Are the sentences true (T) or false (F)?

1 The first people to leave bubblegum in the alley were artists. *F*
2 At first, some people tried to clean the walls in the alley.
3 Everybody loves Bubblegum Alley.
4 The Upside Down House represents what the artist thinks is wrong in the world.
5 You go into the house through a window.
6 The TV is in the living room.

Listening

1 🔊 **2.22** Listen to the radio interview. Complete the sentence.

The most unusual place Troy has ever stayed in is in .... .

🔊 Listening Bank Unit 5 page 119

2 Think about a tourist attraction in your country.

1 Where is it?
2 What is it?
3 What is it like? Describe it.
4 How long has it been a tourist attraction?
5 Who visits the place and why? What do people think of it?

Writing   A travel guide

1   Read the Writing File.

> **Writing File**   Making your writing more interesting
>
> • Use different adjectives to make your writing more interesting.
>
> • Use new vocabulary you have learnt too. It's a good way to remember new words!

2   Read the travel guide. Find the opposites of these adjectives.

1 large *small*
2 unfriendly
3 rainy
4 ugly
5 unknown
6 terrible

Travel Guide

Brighton

destination

Travel Guide: My city by Hayley West

My home city is Brighton. It's a small city, near the sea, in the south of England. I love living in Brighton because the people are friendly and the weather is often sunny. There are also lots of music festivals there.

There are many things to see and do in Brighton. One of the main attractions is Brighton Pavilion. It's a beautiful palace and it's more than two hundred years old! Another famous attraction is Brighton Pier. There's a fantastic funfair there. After you have seen the sights, you can sit in a beach café or buy some souvenirs. If you enjoy watersports, you can go windsurfing or sailing, too. Brighton is a lovely city and has a lot to offer. When you visit Brighton, get a newspaper and see what's on. You might have a nice surprise!

3   Find the adjectives in these sentences. Then copy and complete the table.

1 Oxford is a small city, but it's very busy.
2 There are lots of great tourist attractions there.
3 The most popular attraction is the university.
4 There's an interesting museum and a famous library, too.
5 People are usually helpful and friendly.
6 The weather is often rainy and cold.

Town/City	*small, busy*
People	
Weather	
Tourist attractions	

4   Read the travel guide again. Answer the questions.

1 Where is Brighton? *It's in the south of England.*
2 What are the people like there?
3 What is the weather like?
4 What are the main attractions?
5 What can you do at the beach?
6 How can you find out what's happening in Brighton?

5   Think about your town. Answer the questions. Make notes.

1 Where is it?
2 What do you think of it?
3 What are the people like?
4 Is the weather usually good or bad?
5 Are there any famous or unusual tourist attractions?
6 What activities can you do there?

6   Write a travel guide. Use 'My favourite town/ city' and your notes from Exercise 5.

> **My favourite town/city**
>
> 1 Introduce your town/city
> 2 Describe what you can see and do
> 3 Give your conclusion

> **Remember!**
> • Use different adjectives to make your writing more interesting.
> • Use the vocabulary in this unit.
> • Check your grammar, spelling and punctuation.

Refresh Your Memory!

Grammar Review

1 Match the beginnings (1–8) to the endings (a–h) of the sentences.

1 They've been on holiday for *b*
2 He's lived in Spain since
3 I waited two hours for
4 She hasn't written her travel blog for
5 I haven't worn a T-shirt since
6 We've tried lots of different sports since
7 They haven't had a sunny day for
8 I haven't received a text message since

a a long time. She's got a lot to write about.
b three weeks. They don't want to go home.
c he was a child. He speaks fluent Spanish.
d weeks. It's been very cloudy.
e last weekend. I miss my friends!
f we arrived. We've been very busy!
g a train this morning. I was fed up.
h Monday. It's too cold!

2 Complete the sentences. Use *just* and these verbs.

arrive	buy	eat	~~finish~~
get	have	miss	pass

1 Sorry, there isn't any more pizza. We*'ve just finished* it.
2 They .... some souvenirs. They haven't got any more money.
3 That was the postman. I .... a postcard.
4 He's very tired. He .... home.
5 She's upset. She .... an argument with her mother.
6 I .... my exam. I'm very happy!
7 We .... the last bus. We'll have to walk home.
8 I .... the last slice of bread. I'll have to go to the supermarket later.

Vocabulary Review

3 Complete the sentences with these verbs.

buy	get	lost	packed
~~put up~~	stay	went (x2)	write

1 We arrived at the campsite, *put up* our tent, then made a cup of tea.
2 Have you .... your bag? Yes, I'm ready to go.
3 I sometimes .... a travel blog on holiday.
4 If we take a map with us, we won't .... lost.
5 He doesn't .... souvenirs on holiday because he never has enough money.
6 When we .... abroad last year, we .... our luggage at the airport.
7 We usually .... in a hotel, but this year we .... camping.

4 Match the meanings of *get* (a–f) to the sentences (1–6).

a arrive *2*   d fetch
b buy   e become
c receive   f walk/move

1 I **got** your text message this morning. What's the matter?
2 I was late for school this morning. I **got** there at half past nine!
3 Can you **get** the football? It's in the car.
4 He **got** a new computer game with his birthday money.
5 School exams **are getting** more and more difficult.
6 When the school bus arrived, we all **got** on.

Speaking Review

5 **2.23** **Put the conversation in the correct order. Then listen and check.**

a No, it's only five minutes on foot.
b Excuse me. Can you help me? *1*
c There's a good souvenir shop on Weymouth Street.
d Where's a good place to buy postcards?
e Sure.
f Is it far?

Dictation

6 **2.24** **Listen and write in your notebook.**

✓ **My assessment profile:** Workbook page 131

Literature File

Gulliver's Travels

by: Jonathan Swift

Introduction

It's 1726 and Gulliver is travelling across the sea from England. There's a storm and his boat is shipwrecked. He arrives in a strange country called Lilliput. He meets very small people there. Later, he travels to other countries and meets very big people and horses. They all ask Gulliver about his country and how it is different. Are people better or worse there? Are they good or bad? Gulliver returns home, but his adventures have changed his ideas and his life.

···· Chapter 1 – I came to Lilliput ····

I woke up after nine hours. It was daylight and I was on my back. I tried to stand up, but I could not move! I turned my head a little and looked around me. I saw thousands of strings across my body. … Then something moved on my foot. It moved over my body and up to my face. I looked down and saw a man. He was smaller than my hand. Forty more little men followed him … The man began to speak. His words were strange to me, but I watched his hands. 'We will not hurt you,' I understood. 'But do not try and run away, or we will kill you.' I put up my hand and showed him: 'I will stay here.' Then I had an idea. I also put my hand to my mouth: 'I am hungry.' The man understood me. He shouted to the people on the ground. A hundred men climbed onto my body and walked up to my mouth. They carried food for me. It came from the king they told me later.

Reading

1 Look at the photo of Gulliver from the book *Gulliver's Travels*. Answer the questions.

  1 Where is he?
  2 What is happening?
  3 How do you think the little people feel?

2 Read the Introduction and the extract from Chapter 1 quickly. Were your predictions correct?

3 🔊 2.25 Read the Introduction again. Choose the correct option.

  1 Gulliver goes to Lilliput *on holiday / by accident*.
  2 He meets *very big / very small* people there.
  3 He meets horses *in the same place / in another country*.
  4 After his adventures, Gulliver *changes / doesn't change* his life.

Gulliver's boat is shipwrecked.

4 🔊 2.26 Read the extract from Chapter 1. Answer the questions.

  1 What happened when Gulliver woke up?
  He tried to stand up, but he couldn't move because he was tied up.
  2 How are the Lilliputians different from Gulliver?
  3 How many men were on Gulliver?
  4 How does Gulliver talk to the little man?
  5 How do the people help him?
  6 What type of ruler does Lilliput have?

My Literature File

5 Make notes about a book you have read. It can be about a journey, or an experience of a strange new place. Think about:

- when the story happens
- where events happen
- who is/are the main character(s)
- new places they go to
- new people they meet
- what happens in the end

6 Write an Introduction to the book. Add photos or pictures. Use your notes from Exercise 5 to help you.

6 That's Life!

Grammar	*have to, don't have to, must, mustn't*; Predictions with *will, won't, might*
Vocabulary	Household chores; Feelings adjectives
Speaking	Giving advice (*should, shouldn't*)
Writing	A problem page

Vocabulary   Household chores

1   ◆)) 2.27   **Match the pictures (1–16) to these words. Then listen, check and repeat.**

clear the table	cook a meal
do the ironing	do the washing-up
feed the cat	hang out the washing
lay the table	load the dishwasher
make your bed *1*	mow the lawn
run the washing machine	sweep the floor
take out the rubbish	walk the dog
wash the car	vacuum the floor

Word list page 77   **Workbook** page 109

2   **Complete the sentences with the household chores from Exercise 1.**

1 First, *cook a meal* and *lay the table*. Then you can eat.

2 .... with all the dirty plates or, if you haven't got a dishwasher, ... after the meal.

3 If there are bits of food under the table, ... or .... .

4 When you have dirty clothes, ... and then .... in the sun to dry.

5 Before you wear your clothes again, ...

6 When the bin in the kitchen is full, ...

7 .... every day. Pets can't live without food.

8 When the grass is too long, ...

9 .... every day. These pets need lots of exercise.

10 .... on the drive so it looks nice and clean.

3   **In pairs, ask and answer.**

1 What chores do you do at mealtimes?

I always lay and clear the table and I sometimes cook dinner on Saturdays.

2 What chores do other people in your family do?

3 What other chores do you do in the house?

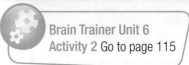

Brain Trainer Unit 6
Activity 2 Go to page 115

Reading

1 Read the webpage quickly. Choose the best title.

  1 The world's laziest teenager
  2 Teens work harder than their parents
  3 Today's teens don't do chores

2))) **2.28** Read the webpage again. Are these sentences true (T) or false (F)?

  1 Cleaning the bathroom is a more popular chore with teenagers than doing the ironing. *F*
  2 More than half of all teenagers have never cooked a meal.
  3 Dr Sheila Green thinks teenagers are lazy.
  4 She thinks teenagers will be good at their jobs.
  5 Dan Sparks thinks teenagers do a lot of homework.
  6 He thinks it's more important that teenagers do homework, sport and music than chores.
  7 Linda Fiorelli makes her children do chores.
  8 Linda Fiorelli thinks children don't learn anything when they do chores.

3 **What about you?** In pairs, ask and answer.

  1 How much free time do you have every day?
  2 How much time do you spend on household chores?
  3 Do you think you do a fair share of the household chores? Why?/Why not?

> *How much free time do you have every day?*

> *Not much – I do a lot of sport after school.*

> *I have a lot of free time – about two or three hours I think.*

TeenWorld.co.com/uk

← → C ⌂

A study of British teenagers has found that most of them have never done any household chores. Many young people aged 11 to 16 don't have to make their bed. Thirty-five percent have never cooked a meal, sixty-three percent have never done the ironing and more than seventy-five percent have never run the washing machine or cleaned the bathroom.

Dr Sheila Green is one of the writers of the study. 'This information is very worrying.' she says.

'Every year, teenagers are getting lazier. Real jobs in the real world will be very difficult for them.'

Dan Sparks, from the parents' website FamilyFirst.com, disagrees. 'Young people today work very hard – harder than their parents, sometimes. Many of them have to do three hours of homework every night. Playing in a sports team or learning a musical instrument can take a lot of time, too and these activities are an important part of teenagers' lives. If we want young people with good exam results and also some interests outside school, we mustn't give them chores.'

Linda Fiorelli, writer of *The Happy Home,* feels very differently. 'It's about respect, not time. Even my five-year-old son has to lay the table every day. It takes one minute, but it's important. Children share the house with their parents, so they must share the jobs around the house, too. That's fair and it teaches good habits for the future.'

Grammar *have to/don't have to*

Affirmative

I/You/We/They have to lay the table.
He/She/It has to lay the table.

Negative

I/You/We/They don't have to lay the table.
He/She/It doesn't have to lay the table.

Questions and short answers

Do you have to do any chores?
Yes, I do./No, I don't.

Does he have to do any chores?
Yes, he does./No, he doesn't.

Grammar reference Workbook page 96

1 Study the grammar table. Choose the correct options to complete the rules.

> **1** We use *have to* when something *is / isn't* necessary.
> **2** We use *don't have to* when something *is / isn't* necessary.

2 Find more examples in the article on page 65.

3 Make sentences and questions.
  1 clear / the table / has / She / to
  She has to clear the table.

  2 the dog / don't / to / We / have / walk
  3 I / Do / do / have / any chores / to / ?
  4 doesn't / vacuum / the floor / He / to / have
  5 They / the washing / to / hang out / have
  6 go / Why / you / have / to / do / ?

4 Complete the sentences. Use the verbs and the correct form of *have to*.
  1 We *have to tidy* (tidy) our bedroom every week.
  2 My parents .... (not cook) dinner tonight. We're going to a restaurant.
  3 He .... (help) me! I can't do it on my own.
  4 I'm really dirty! I .... (have) a shower before I go out.
  5 .... (they/do) any homework tonight?
  6 My sister .... (not make) her bed in the morning because she's only three.

5 Make questions with *have to*.
  1 Clara and David / cook dinner?
  Do Clara and David have to cook dinner?

  2 Mum / clean the living room?
  3 Dad / feed the cat?
  4 Clara and David / load the dishwasher?
  5 Clara / wash the car?
  6 David / tidy his bedroom?

6 Look at the note. Answer the questions in Exercise 5.
  1 *No, they don't. Dad has to cook dinner.*

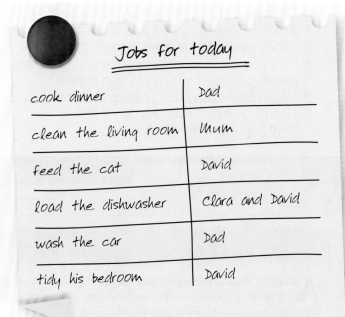

Jobs for today

cook dinner	Dad
clean the living room	Mum
feed the cat	David
load the dishwasher	Clara and David
wash the car	Dad
tidy his bedroom	David

must/mustn't

Obligation

I must leave now. It's late.
I have to help my mum.

No obligation

I don't have to cook any meals.

Prohibition

You mustn't talk in the library.

Grammar reference Workbook page 96

7 Study the grammar table. Do these words mean the same thing?
  1 *must* and *have to*
  2 *mustn't* and *don't have to*

8 Replace the words in bold in each sentence so they have the same meaning. Use these words.

I don't have to	I have to	~~I must~~	I mustn't

1 **I have to** take out the rubbish. *I must* take out the rubbish.
2 **It isn't necessary to** mow the lawn.
3 **I must** do a lot of chores.
4 **I can't** swim here.

9 Choose the correct options.

I'm in a swimming team and it's hard work. We
¹ *must / doesn't have to* swim for an hour before
school. I ² *must / have to* get up at 6 a.m. because
school starts at 8.30 and we ³ *mustn't / don't have to*
be late for class! We ⁴ *mustn't / have to* practise every
morning from Monday to Friday. On Saturdays there
are competitions and we ⁵ *must / don't have to* be
fast if we want to stay in the team. On Sundays there
aren't any competitions, so we ⁶ *mustn't / don't have
to* go to the swimming pool. I love Sundays!

10 Make true sentences about your country. Use
the correct form of *must, mustn't, have to* or
don't have to.

1 When you're two years old, you .... go
to school.
2 Students .... be polite to their teachers.
3 You .... use your mobile phone in class.
4 We .... wear school uniform.
5 You .... throw rubbish in the street.

Pronunciation /ʌ/ and /juː/

11a)) 2.29 **Listen and repeat. Think about
the pronunciation of the underlined *u*.**

am<u>u</u>sing	conf<u>u</u>sed	d<u>u</u>ll	<u>u</u>pset
<u>u</u>nder	<u>u</u>sually		

b)) 2.30 **Listen and repeat. Then practise
saying the sentences.**

1 He uses rubbish to make statues.
2 Some of us watched a funny documentary
at the museum.
3 Tuesday was a beautiful, sunny summer's day.
4 My mum made some disgusting tuna
sandwiches for lunch.

Vocabulary Feelings adjectives

1)) 2.31 **Look at these words. Check the
meaning in a dictionary. Listen and repeat.**

confident	confused	disappointed	embarrassed
fed up	glad	grateful	guilty
jealous	lonely	nervous	relaxed
relieved	upset		

> **Word list** page 77   **Workbook** page 109

2 Match the sentences to the words from Exercise 1.

1 I was really worried, but now everything's OK.
  relieved
2 It's not fair! Why can't I have that?
3 I was hoping for a better result.
4 Thank you so much!
5 My exam starts in a minute. Help!
6 My exam starts in a minute. I think I can do well in it.
7 No one ever talks to me.
8 I'm so sorry I did that to you.

3 Read the short texts. How do the people feel?
Make sentences using these words.

confused	embarrassed	~~fed up~~	glad	guilty
jealous	~~nervous~~	relaxed	upset	

1 It's Sam's first day at a new school. He's been
to three different schools in the last three years.
  *Sam is nervous and he's fed up because he
  often has to change school.*
2 Ginny thinks she sees her friend in the street. She
runs up to him and says hello. But this person is
Connor and he's never met Ginny before.
3 Jack loves Emily and Emily loves Jack, but
Sophie loves Jack, too. She cries when she
sees him. Jack wants Sophie to be happy.
4 Ben doesn't have to do anything today, so he's
lying in the sun. It's a beautiful day.

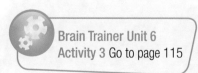

Brain Trainer Unit 6
Activity 3 Go to page 115

Chatroom Giving advice

Speaking and Listening

1 **Look at the photo. Answer the questions.**

1 Who has got a problem?
2 What do you think it is?

2 🔊 **2.32** **Listen and read the conversation. Check your answers.**

3 🔊 **2.32** **Listen and read again. Choose the correct options.**

1 Ruby *is / isn't* happy.
2 She *has / hasn't* finished her homework.
3 She usually does her homework *at the weekend / on school nights*.
4 She *has to / doesn't have to* do chores on school nights.
5 *Ruby / Ruby's parents* usually walk(s) the dog.
6 Ruby *goes / doesn't go* to climbing club.

4 **Act out the conversation in groups of three.**

Tom	What's wrong, Ruby? You look a bit fed up.
Ruby	I am. I've done six hours of homework today!
Tom	Maybe you should have a rest.
Ruby	A rest? I wish! I haven't even started my Maths and that'll be really hard …
Ella	You won't have any problems with it, I'm sure. You're great at Maths! But maybe you shouldn't do all your homework at the weekend, Ruby.
Ruby	I haven't got enough time for homework on school nights.
Ella	Why don't you talk to your parents about your chores? Maybe they can walk the dog in the evening and you can study.
Ruby	No, they're too busy. I might stop going to climbing club so I have more time.
Tom	I don't think you should stop climbing, Ruby. You love it!

Say it in your language …
What's wrong?
I wish!

5 Look back at the conversation. Complete these sentences.

1 Maybe you *should* have a rest.
2 Maybe you .... do all your homework at the weekend.
3 Why .... you talk to your parents about your chores?
4 I don't .... you should stop climbing.

6 Read the phrases for giving advice.

Positive	Negative
Maybe you should …	Maybe you shouldn't …
I think you should …	I don't think you should …
Why don't you …?	

7 🔊 2.33 Listen to the conversation. What two pieces of advice does Tom give Ella? Act out the conversation in pairs.

Ella I can't ¹ find my school jumper!
Tom Why don't you ² tidy your room?
Ella No, I can't do that. ³ I haven't got time now. I know! I can ⁴ wear your jumper.
Tom I don't think you should do that. ⁵ It's too big. Maybe you should ⁶ borrow a jumper from Ruby.

8 Work in pairs. Replace the words in purple in Exercise 7. Use these words and/or your own ideas. Act out the conversations.

I can't find my mobile phone!

Why don't you look in the living room?

1 do my homework / find a present for Mum / sleep at night

2 ask your teacher for help / buy that bag / read a book in bed

3 He/She never helps. / I can't afford it. / I hate reading.

4 copy your homework / give her a pen / buy a nicer bed

5 You're too lazy. / It's too boring. / It's too expensive.

6 work harder / look for something at the market / drink hot chocolate before bed

Grammar Predictions with *will, won't, might*

Definite
I think she'll be relieved.
You won't have any problems, I'm sure.
Will they finish it?

Possible
I might see them tomorrow. I'm not sure.
He might not like the film.

Watch Out!
will not = won't
might not = ~~mightn't~~

▷ Grammar reference Workbook page 96

1 Study the grammar table. Complete the rules with *will* or *might*.

1 We use .... when we are sure about something in the future.
2 We use .... when we aren't sure about something in the future.
3 The contracted form of .... is *'ll*.
4 The contracted form of .... is *won't*.

2 Choose the correct options in Ruby's predictions.

1 Ella and Tom *will / might* come to the cinema with me. They haven't decided.
2 Ash *won't / might not* like the film. He hates romantic comedies.
3 Bad weather *won't / might not* be a problem at an indoor swimming pool.
4 I'm sure the Maths test *will / might* be difficult.
5 I *won't / might not* pass the test. I can't be sure.

3 Complete the predictions. Use *will* or *might* and contracted forms where possible.

1 One day I*'ll be* (be) famous. I feel very confident about that.
2 My team .... (win) the match. We're quite good, but the other team is quite good too.
3 I .... (not finish) my English homework tonight. I'm not sure.
4 They think he .... (arrive) after lunch.
5 .... (you/have) time to wash the car?

Reading

1 Look at the picture of a teenager of the future. How is his life different from the lives of teenagers today?

What sort of life will teenagers have fifty years from now? No one can be sure, but experts have made some interesting predictions.

1 The home
Robots will make the beds, sweep the floor and hang out the washing, so teenagers won't have to do many chores. Parents and teenagers might have a more relaxed relationship because of this. Or will they just find other things to argue about?

2 School
Some people might travel to school, but most people will study on their home computers and have virtual lessons with the world's best teachers. One teacher might have a million students! All the lessons will be in English and everyone around the world will take the same exams.

3 Free time
Teenagers won't go to cafés and cinemas with friends, but they won't be lonely. They'll have fun in a virtual world and go to amazing virtual parties with their favourite stars.

4 Entertainment
The films of today will seem very boring because you can't change the story as you watch. In fifty years, all entertainment will be interactive – there will be no difference between video games and films.

5 Fashion
Teenagers will be fatter than today because they won't do much exercise, so the most popular clothes will be very big and baggy. Global warming will bring changes in fashion, too. There will be air conditioning inside a lot of clothes – a big help in the hot temperatures around the world.

In fifty years, you will be old and grey. What will you think of the teens of the future?

Key Words	
relationship	argue
virtual	baggy
global warming	air conditioning

2 Read the magazine article and check your answer to Exercise 1.

3 ◗)) 2.34 Read these headings. Which paragraph do you think will mention these things? Read the article quickly to check.

clothes 5	chores	exams	parents
parties	languages	video games	

4 ◗)) 2.34 Read the article again. Answer the questions.

1 Why might parents and their teenage children have a better relationship in the future?

Because robots will do the teenagers' chores.

2 How will a normal lesson in the future be different from a normal lesson today? Find three differences.
3 Will teenagers enjoy their free time?
4 What will their parties be like?
5 What will future teenagers think of our films?
6 What two reasons does the article give for the changes in fashion?

5 Which predictions in the article do you think are:

1 correct?   **2** silly?   **3** exciting?   **4** scary?

'There will be no difference between video games and films.' I think that's correct, because it's starting to happen now.

Listening

1 ◗)) 2.35 Listen to some teenagers of the future. Match the conversations (1–4) to the topics (A–D).

A the home
B school
C free time
D fashion

◗))) Listening Bank Unit 6 page 119

Writing   A problem page

1 **Read the Writing File.**

- You can introduce a reason with *because*.
  I feel guilty because I broke my dad's mobile.

- You can introduce a result with *so*.
  I broke my dad's mobile, so he's really angry with me.

2 **Read the problem page from a magazine. Find the linking words of reason and result.**

Problem page

My mum works in a restaurant on Saturday nights, so I have to look after my six-year-old sister. All my friends have fun together then, but I can't be with them. It isn't fair! What should I do?
Tilly

I'm sure your mum is very grateful for your help on Saturdays, but you should talk to her about your problem. Choose a time when she isn't busy because it'll be easier to think of an answer to the problem then. For example, someone else might be happy to look after your sister some weeks. Other weeks, invite some friends to your house. You'll have more fun at home with your friends there. Cook them some nice food and watch a film together. But remember, you mustn't make a lot of noise because your sister has to sleep. And always tidy the house when they've gone, so your mum doesn't have to do any household chores after a long evening at work.
You and your mum might have lots of other good ideas, too. Good luck!

3 **Complete the sentences with *because* or *so*.**

1 I'm tired *because* I went to bed late last night.
2 He's jealous of his sister .... she's better at sport than him.
3 You've finished your homework, ... now you can watch a DVD.
4 I didn't do well in the race, ... I'm a bit disappointed.
5 She's really upset .... her best friend shouted at her.

4 **Read the problem page again. Answer the questions.**

1 Who should Tilly talk to about her problem? When?
   She should talk to her mum when she isn't busy.
2 What idea does the writer have so that Tilly can go out with her friends?
3 What idea does the writer have so that Tilly can have more fun at home?
4 What two pieces of advice does the writer give about the second idea?

5 **Read about James' problem. Answer the questions. Make notes.**

I moved to a new town last year. I've got a lot of friends around the world because I play online games in my free time, but everyone at school is really unfriendly. I'm starting to feel quite lonely. How can I make new friends here?
James

1 Is it normal to feel lonely in James' situation?
2 Should he talk to anyone about his problem? Who?
3 Are school friends more important than online friends? Why?/Why not?
4 What can he do to make friends at school?
5 How do you think he'll feel after a few months?

6 **Write a letter giving advice to James. Use 'My letter' and your notes from Exercise 5.**

My letter

Paragraph 1
General advice for this problem
Paragraph 2
Specific ideas that might help
Paragraph 3
Encouraging ending

Remember!
- Use linking words for reason and result.
- Use the vocabulary in this unit.
- Check your grammar, spelling and punctuation.

Refresh Your Memory!

Grammar Review

1 **Make sentences and questions with *have to*.**

1 we / learn English at school
   We have to learn English at school.
2 you / study French?
3 my sister / not / do any homework
4 she / practise the piano every day
5 she / do any chores?
6 I / get up early for school
7 my parents / not / start work early

2 **Complete the text with these words.**

don't	~~have~~	has	must	mustn't	to

My brother and I ¹ ***have*** to stay with my
grandparents this week. It's fun, but they have a
lot of rules. For example, we ² .... use our mobile
phones in the house because they hate mobile
phones. I ³ .... call my friends on the home phone.
My brother ⁴ .... to walk the dog every day, but I ⁵ ....
have to do that because I've got a bad leg. I have
⁶ .... help Granny with the cooking and ironing instead.

3 **Complete the conversation. Use *will, won't* or *might* and the verbs.**

A   Do you want to come to the Smugglers concert
    on Saturday? I'm sure you ¹ ***will enjoy*** (enjoy) it.
B   I ² .... (not be) here on Saturday, so I can't
    come with you.
A   Where ³ .... (you/be)?
B   In the mountains with my cousins.
A   The weather forecast says it ⁴ .... (snow) in the
    mountains at the weekend. They're not sure.
B   Cool! We ⁵ .... (go) snowboarding then, or we
    ⁶ .... (not do) anything. It's horrible outside
    when it's too cold and windy.

Vocabulary Review

4 **Match the beginnings (1–7) to the endings
(a–g) of the sentences.**

1 You should walk   a the rubbish.
2 She never does   b the dog.
3 Please can you mow   c the ironing.
4 Remember to feed   d the lawn?
5 I don't have to wash   e the cat.
6 You didn't run   f the washing machine.
7 We have to take out   g the car.

5 **Complete the sentences with the correct
feelings adjectives.**

1 I like Mr Green. I'm **glad** he's our teacher.
2 I'm really n _ _ _ _ _ _ about tomorrow's concert.
   I might forget the words to all the songs!
3 I think someone's stolen my purse! Oh no, it's
   here. I'm so r _ _ _ _ _ _ _ !
4 You've really helped me. I'm so g _ _ _ _ _ _ _ .
5 I said some terrible things to her. I feel really
   g _ _ _ _ _ about that now.
6 I want to be rich. I'm so j _ _ _ _ _ _ of people
   with lots of money.
7 I'm sure I can do it. I'm feeling very c _ _ _ _ _ _ _ _ .

Speaking Review

6 🔊 **2.36** **Complete the advice for these
situations. Then listen and check.**

1 A I'm late for school again!
   B Why ***don't you*** get up earlier?
2 A I want to go to Antarctica on holiday.
   B I .... you should do that. You hate cold weather!
3 A When I sweep the floor, it takes hours!
   B Maybe .... vacuum the floor instead.
4 A I'm feeling quite relaxed about the exams.
   B I .... should be more worried. They're
     very important!
5 A When I load the dishwasher, I usually break
     a plate.
   B Maybe .... do your chores so quickly.

Dictation

7 🔊 **2.37** **Listen and write in your notebook.**

✓ **My assessment profile:** Workbook page 132

Real World Profiles

Rob Frenette's Profile

Age:
23 years old

Home country:
Canada

My favourite things …

writing my blog, helping others, working with BullyingCanada

Reading

1 **Read Rob's profile and look at the photos. Correct the mistakes in this sentence. Then read the article quickly to check.**

Rob lives in the USA and has started a newspaper for people with bullying problems.

2 🔊 **2.38** **Read the article again. Answer the questions.**

1 How did Rob often feel at school? Why?

He felt lonely and scared because he had problems with bullies.

2 Why did he first talk to a newspaper?
3 What help can people find on Rob's website?
4 Why does Rob travel around Canada a lot?
5 What advice does he give to people with bullying problems?
6 What is Blue Day?

Rob's story

For more than eleven years, Rob Frenette had problems with bullies at school. He was often lonely and scared. When he was fifteen, however, he decided to do something about his problems. He walked into a newspaper office and told them about the bullying. His story went into the newspaper and soon all the TV stations in Canada wanted to talk to him about his experiences. They also wanted to hear his ideas to stop bullying.

After that, Rob continued his studies at school, but in his free time he helped other people with bullying problems. With a friend Katie Neu, he made a website called www.bullyingcanada.ca. Visitors to the website can find advice, stories and poems about bullying, in both English and French. When people are upset, they can chat on the phone or online to Rob and his team. Every weekend Rob has to answer emails to the website. He also speaks to children, teachers and politicians around the country about bullying.

Rob's most important message is: 'When bullies are unkind to you, it isn't your fault. There's nothing wrong with you, so you should try to stay confident. And remember that people care about your problems. You just have to find those people.'

One of Rob's ideas is 'Blue Day', a special anti-bullying day in schools. Students have to wear blue clothes and in class they learn how to stop bullying. More than 150 Canadian schools now celebrate Blue Day, but Rob won't stop until there's a Blue Day in every school in Canada.

Key Words

| bullies | bullying | fault |
| celebrate | until | |

Class discussion

1 Are there problems with bullying in your country?
2 Are there any websites to help young people with bullying problems?
3 What other help can these people get?

Grammar   Present perfect

1 **Complete the sentences with the Present perfect form of the verbs.**

1 *Have* you *ever been* (be) to Russia?
2 No. But I .... (always want) to go there.
3 I .... (never try) Japanese food.
4 Kelly .... (not finish) her project.
5 My brother .... (always want) to be a pilot.
6 The students .... (not do) their homework again.
7 .... you .... (hear) the news? We .... (win) the tournament!
8 Where .... you .... (be)? I .... (not see) you for a long time.

Present perfect vs Past simple

2 **Complete the conversations with the Present perfect or Past simple form of the verbs.**

1
A ¹ *Have* you *ever ridden* (ride) a camel?
B Yes, I ² .... (ride) one. I ³ .... (take) a trip through the desert in Morocco once.
A When ⁴ .... you .... (go) to Morocco?
B We ⁵ .... (spend) a week there last year.

2
A When ⁶ .... you .... (come) back from holiday?
B I ⁷ .... (fly) back last night.
A What ⁸ .... (be) it like?
B Great! ⁹ .... you .... (ever go) to Florida?
A No, I ¹⁰ .... (not).

Present perfect + *for* and *since*, *How long?*

3 **Make sentences with *How long*? Complete the answers with *for* or *since*.**

1 A you / live / in this house?
   How long have you lived in this house?
2 B .... I was a child – so, ... fifteen years!
3 A your father / work / in the bank?
4 B .... five years.
5 A you have / the same hairstyle?
6 B .... I was about six!
7 A you know / your best friend?
8 B .... three years.
9 A your class / study / English?
10 B .... we were at primary school.

Present perfect with *just*

4 **Complete the sentences with *just* and the Present perfect.**

1 A Something smells delicious in your kitchen. *Have you just baked* a cake? (bake)
2 B Yes! I .... it out of the oven. (take)
3 I'm really tired. I .... for a run around the park. (go)
4 Stella .... back from holiday. (arrive)
5 I .... my Maths homework – after two hours! (finish)
6 I'm crying, because I .... a sad film on TV. (watch)

have to/don't have to

5 **Rewrite the sentences using the correct form of *have to* or *don't have to*.**

1 It's essential to wear a helmet on a bike.
   You have to wear a helmet.
2 It's not essential to book tickets in advance.
   You .... tickets in advance.
3 Swimmers need swimming caps. It's a rule.
   Swimmers .... swimming caps.
4 You can sit down if you are tired.
   You .... stand.
5 You aren't allowed to arrive late.
   You .... on time.
6 You can have lunch at school or at home. It's your choice.
   You .... have lunch at school.

must/mustn't

6 **Make rules with *must* or *mustn't* for these signs.**

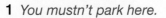

1 *You mustn't park here.*

Predictions with *will, won't, might*

7 **Choose the correct option.**

1 Look at those black storm clouds. It *won't / will* rain later.

2 I'm not sure if I'm going to Mark's party. I *will / might* go.

3 They've been together for ages. I'm sure they *might / will* get married.

4 It's been decided. Italy *might / will* play Spain in the finals.

5 This answer *might / will* be right. I'm not too sure about it.

6 I promise – I *might not / won't* tell anyone your secret.

Speaking   Doubt and disbelief

1 **Complete the conversation with these words.**

believe	impossible	~~joking~~	really

A Have you heard about this amazing coincidence? A man was walking under a window at the top of a building, when a baby fell out.

B You're [1] *joking*!

A No, it's true. And he was passing at just the right time, so he caught the baby in his arms!

B No, [2] .... ?

A Yes, I read it in the paper. And then the same thing happened a few years later.

B I don't [3] .... it.

A It happened to the same man, outside the same building!

B That's [4] .... !

A I know, it's the strangest thing.

Asking for information

2 **Put the conversation in the correct order.**

1. Excuse me, can you help me? I'm looking for the museum. Do you know where it is?

.... It's a nice walk from here, or you can get a bus.

.... Yes, I do. It's just across the river, on the left.

.... Oh yes, there are lots of restaurants and cafés.

.... I'd like to walk. But is it far?

.... OK, so we have to cross the river. How can we get to the river?

.... That doesn't sound too far. And are there any nice places to eat near there?

.... No, it's about twenty minutes on foot.

Giving advice

3 **Complete the conversation with these phrases.**

I don't think you should worry	Maybe you should tell
~~Why don't you talk~~	You shouldn't pretend

A What's wrong? You look really upset.

B I feel awful about my Science exam results. I don't know how I'm going to tell my parents I did so badly. But I'm really bad at Science and I want to do Drama instead.

A [1] *Why don't you talk* to your parents about it?

B The trouble is, they think I really like it.

A [2] .... them the truth.

B They'll be upset. After all, they're both doctors.

A [3] .... about that. They'll understand. [4] .... you're interested in something when you aren't.

B Yes, perhaps you're right.

Vocabulary   News and media

1 **Match the phrases (1–8) to their definitions (a–h).**

1 an online diary *h*

2 the title of a newspaper article

3 a formal question and answer session with a person

4 a sudden news announcement

5 a person who writes newspaper articles

6 a newspaper article

7 a person who gives the news on TV

8 a news programme that can be downloaded on an MP3 player

a interview

b journalist

c headline

d news flash

e news presenter

f podcast

g report

h blog

Adverbs of manner

2 Complete the sentences with these adverbs.

angrily	carefully	early	fast	late
loudly	~~quietly~~	sadly		

1 Please enter the room *quietly* – students are writing exams.
2 Can you speak more .... ? I can't hear you – it's very noisy in here.
3 Please drive .... – the roads are dangerous.
4 He's a fantastic athlete. He can run so .... .
5 'Go away,' he said, quietly but .... .
6 I thought it would be a funny film, but it ended so .... , I cried.
7 If you don't get up soon, you'll arrive at school .... for your lessons.
8 It's best to arrive .... – then we'll get the best seats in the cinema.

Holidays

3 Match the verbs (1–8) to the words (a–h) to make holiday phrases.

1 book		**a**	a travel blog
2 eat		**b**	camping
3 go		**c**	in a hotel
4 pack		**d**	a holiday
5 stay		**e**	a tent
6 get		**f**	a tan
7 put up		**g**	your bag
8 write		**h**	out

Meanings of *get*

4 Replace *get* with a different verb with the same meaning.

1 When my parents <u>get</u> old, I'll look after them.
   When my parents become old, I'll look after them.
2 Can you <u>get</u> some milk when you go to the shop?
3 What time will we <u>get</u> home?
4 Did you <u>get</u> an email from Laura about her party?
5 <u>Get</u> off the bus when you see a big grey building in front of you.
6 The dog ran very fast to <u>get</u> the ball.

Household chores

5 Match the verbs (1–8) to the words (a–h) to make household chores.

1 clear		**a**	the floor
2 do		**b**	the bed
3 make		**c**	the dog
4 load		**d**	the table
5 mow		**e**	the rubbish
6 sweep		**f**	the lawn
7 take out		**g**	the ironing
8 walk		**h**	the dishwasher

Feelings adjectives

6 Complete the sentences with these adjectives.

confident	confused	disappointed	glad
grateful	~~jealous~~	nervous	upset

1 Don't be *jealous* of people who seem to have more than you have.
2 It's my exam tomorrow but I'm not .... . I worked hard, so I'm very .... I'll do well.
3 Could you explain that to me again? I'm a bit .... .
4 Thank you very much. I'm very .... for your help.
5 Carla's very .... because her cat died.
6 I'm so .... you're back! I missed you.
7 I'm .... that I didn't get the job.

Word list

Unit 4   In The News

News and media

blog	/blɒg/
current affairs programme	/ˌkʌrənt əˈfeəz ˌprəʊɡræm/
headline	/ˈhedlaɪn/
international news	/ˌɪntənæʃənəl ˈnjuːz/
interview (v)	/ˈɪntəvjuː/
journalist	/ˈdʒɜːnəl-əst/
local news	/ˌləʊkəl ˈnjuːz/
national news	/ˌnæʃənəl ˈnjuːz/
news flash	/ˈnjuːz flæʃ/
newspaper	/ˈnjuːspeɪpə/
news presenter	/ˈnjuːz prɪˌzentə/
news website	/ˈnjuːz ˌwebsaɪt/
podcast	/ˈpɒdkɑːst/
report (v, n)	/rɪˈpɔːt/

Adverbs of manner

angrily	/ˈæŋɡrəli/
badly	/ˈbædli/
carefully	/ˈkeəfəli/
carelessly	/ˈkeələsli/
early	/ˈɜːli/
fast	/fɑːst/
happily	/ˈhæpəli/
hard	/hɑːd/
late	/leɪt/
loudly	/ˈlaʊdli/
patiently	/ˈpeɪʃəntli/
quietly	/ˈkwaɪətli/
sadly	/ˈsædli/
slowly	/ˈsləʊli/
well	/wel/

Unit 5   Happy Holidays

Holidays

book a holiday	/ˌbʊk ə ˈhɒlədi, -deɪ/
buy souvenirs	/ˌbaɪ suːvəˈnɪəz, ˈsuːvənɪəz/
check into a hotel	/ˌtʃek ɪntʊ ə həʊˈtel/
eat out	/ˌiːt ˈaʊt/
get a tan	/ɡet ə ˈtæn/
get lost	/ɡet ˈlɒst/
go abroad	/ˌɡəʊ əˈbrɔːd/
go camping	/ˌɡəʊ ˈkæmpɪŋ/
lose your luggage	/ˌluːz jə ˈlʌɡɪdʒ/
pack your bag	/ˌpæk jə ˈbæɡ/
put up a tent	/ˌpʊt ʌp ə ˈtent/
see the sights	/ˌsiː ðə ˈsaɪts/
stay in a hotel	/ˌsteɪ ɪn ə həʊˈtel/
write a travel blog	/ˌraɪt ə ˈtrævəl blɒg/

Meanings of *get*

arrive	/əˈraɪv/
become	/bɪˈkʌm/
buy	/baɪ/
fetch	/fetʃ/
move	/muːv/
receive	/rɪˈsiːv/
walk	/wɔːk/

Unit 6   That's Life!

Household chores

clear the table	/ˌklɪə ðə ˈteɪbəl/
cook a meal	/ˌkʊk ə ˈmiːl/
do the ironing	/ˌduː ði ˈaɪənɪŋ/
do the washing-up	/ˌduː ðə wɒʃɪŋ ˈʌp/
feed the cat	/ˌfiːd ðə ˈkæt/
hang out the washing	/ˌhæŋ aʊt ðə ˈwɒʃɪŋ/
lay the table	/ˌleɪ ðə ˈteɪbəl/
load the dishwasher	/ˌləʊd ðə ˈdɪʃˌwɒʃə/
make your bed	/ˌmeɪk jə ˈbed/
mow the lawn	/ˌməʊ ðə ˈlɔːn/
run the washing machine	/ˌrʌn ðə ˈwɒʃɪŋ məˌʃiːn/
sweep the floor	/ˌswiːp ðə ˈflɔː/
take out the rubbish	/ˌteɪk aʊt ðə ˈrʌbɪʃ/
walk the dog	/ˌwɔːk ðə ˈdɒg/
wash the car	/ˌwɒʃ ðə ˈkɑː/
vacuum the floor	/ˌvækjuəm ðə ˈflɔː, -kjʊm/

Feelings adjectives

confident	/ˈkɒnfədənt/
confused	/kənˈfjuːzd/
disappointed	/ˌdɪsəˈpɔɪntəd/
embarrassed	/ɪmˈbærəst/
fed up	/ˌfed ˈʌp/
glad	/ɡlæd/
grateful	/ˈɡreɪtfəl/
guilty	/ˈɡɪlti/
jealous	/ˈdʒeləs/
lonely	/ˈləʊnli/
nervous	/ˈnɜːvəs/
relaxed	/rɪˈlækst/
relieved	/rɪˈliːvd/
upset	/ˌʌpˈset/

7 Make A Difference

Grammar	*be going to* and *will*; First conditional
Vocabulary	Protest and support; Verb + preposition
Speaking	Persuading
Writing	A formal letter

Vocabulary Protest and support

1 🔊 **3.1** Match the items in the photos (1–12) to these words and phrases. Then listen, check and repeat.

banner	charity	collection
demonstration	donation	fundraising event
march *1*	petition	placard
sit-in	slogan	volunteer

Word list page 111   **Workbook** page 110

2 Complete the sentences with the words in Exercise 1.

1 Students are having a *sit-in* at school today.
2 This T-shirt has got an interesting .... on it.
3 Did you sign the .... against the new road?
4 A .... or placard always has a strong message.
5 We're having a .... for a local charity.
6 They're having a quiz as a .... . They want to make a lot of money.
7 There are lots of .... for the fun run. We've got lots of help.

3 **What about you?** In pairs, ask and answer.

1 Have you ever made a donation to a charity? Which one?
2 Have you ever been a volunteer? Who for?
3 Have you got a T-shirt with a slogan on it? What does the slogan say?
4 Have there been any marches or sit-ins in your town? What were they for?

> *Have you ever made a donation to a charity?*

> *Yes, I have. I've made donations to the World Wide Fund for Nature.*

Brain Trainer Unit 7
Activity 2 Go to page 116

Reading

1 Look at the text and the photos. Answer the questions.

1 What type of text is it? An article, a letter, a leaflet?
2 What do you think is the topic?

2 Read and check your answers to Exercise 1.

3))) 3.2 Read the text again. Match the headings to paragraphs A–D.

1 Why has this happened? *B*
2 What are Elephant Family's plans?
3 What's the problem?
4 How can you help?

4 Read the text again. Answer the questions.

1 Where do Asian elephants live?
 In India, Thailand, Malaysia and Indonesia.
2 How many Asian elephants are there?
3 How do the elephants look for food?
4 Why do people kill the elephants?
5 What are 'elephant corridors'?
6 What type of event is the Elephant Parade?
7 How can you help the charity Elephant Family?

5 In pairs, ask and answer.

1 Do you think the Elephant Parade is a good idea? Why?/Why not?
2 Have there been any outdoor art exhibitions in your city? Describe them.

London Elephant Parade

You don't usually see elephants in big cities, but you'll probably meet one in town this weekend! This summer there are going to be 200 elephant sculptures around London. They're part of an art exhibition called Elephant Parade. Elephant Parade works with the charity Elephant Family. With your help, we're going to save the Asian elephant.

A ....

Today there are only 25,000 Asian elephants in India, Thailand, Malaysia and Indonesia. A hundred years ago there were 200,000 elephants in these countries.

B ....

The elephants are competing with people for food and space. Asian elephants travel from forest to forest, looking for food. Today the forests are getting smaller and the elephants go through villages to get to them. People in the villages protect their land and kill the elephants. In thirty years there won't be any elephants unless we do something.

C ....

The charity Elephant Family is going to make 'elephant corridors'. They're special roads between the forests and elephants can travel safely there. There's already one in India, but we need many more.

D ....

Come and see Elephant Parade. The parade isn't a march, so we won't have banners or slogans. It's a fundraising event. After the exhibition we're going to sell the sculptures. You can buy smaller elephants or T-shirts on our website, or make a donation and sign our petition.

The future is in our hands. Help us save the Asian elephant.

Grammar   *be going to*

Affirmative

There are going to be 200 elephant sculptures.
The charity is going to make elephant corridors.

Negative

There aren't going to be 200 elephant sculptures.
The charity isn't going to make elephant corridors.

Questions and short answers

Are they going to make them?
Yes, they are./No, they aren't.
What are they going to do?

> **Grammar reference** Workbook page 98

1 **Study the grammar table. Choose the correct options to complete the rules.**

> **1** We use **be going to** to talk about *the future / now*.
> **2** **Be going to** introduces *a prediction / a plan*.

2 **Make conversations. Use *going to/not going to*.**

1 A What / you / do at the weekend?
  B I / buy a new T-shirt.

  What are you going to do at the weekend?
  I'm going to buy a new T-shirt.

2 A It's jeans day tomorrow. What / you / wear?
  B Well, I / not wear my school uniform!
3 A They / have / a collection for charity.
  B I / not make / a donation. I haven't got any money.
4 A You / sign the petition against the new supermarket?
  B Yes, I am. I don't agree with it.
5 A My brother / be a volunteer at the school marathon.
  B What he / do?
6 A You / take a banner on the march?
  B Yes, I am. I / write a slogan on it, too.

Pronunciation   *going to*

3a 🔊 **3.3** **Listen to these sentences. In which sentences do you hear *gonna* instead of *going to*?**

1 I'm going to play football.
2 What time is it going to start?
3 We're going to have a concert.
4 Are you going to come to the party?

b 🔊 **3.3** **Listen again and repeat.**

4 🔊 **3.4** **Complete the conversation. Then listen and check.**

A Hey, Connor. ¹ *Are you gonna play* (you/play) football in the park on Saturday?
B No, I'm not. I ² .... (make) a banner.
A What for?
B Sunday is Earth Day. There ³ .... (be) a march.
A Earth Day? ⁴ .... a lot of people .... (go)?
B Yes, they are. And after the march, we ⁵ .... (have) a concert in the park.
A That's cool. Who ⁶ .... (play)?
B Adele and Coldplay.
A Wow! What time ⁷ .... (start)?
B At 3 o'clock. ⁸ .... (you/come)?
A Yes, I am.
B Great. You can help me with my banner!

5 **Imagine you are organising a concert for a charity. In pairs, ask and answer.**

1 Which charity / help?
2 Which group / play?
3 the concert / be at school?
4 What time / start and finish?
5 How / make money? you / sell, T-shirts, CDs?

> *Which charity are you going to help?*
>
> *We're going to help the World Wide Fund for Nature.*

will or *be going to*

Predictions

In 30 years there won't be any Asian elephants.
You'll probably meet one in town this weekend.

Plans or intentions

We're going to save the Asian elephant.

> **Grammar reference** Workbook page 98

6 Look at the sentences. Are they plans or predictions?

1 Your horoscope says: 'The colour red will bring you good luck'. *prediction*
2 I'm not going to go to school tomorrow – it's Saturday!
3 We're going to go to the football match this weekend. We've bought our tickets.
4 I don't think he'll pass his exams. He never does his homework.
5 My friend has problems with Maths, so I'm going to help him after school.
6 I'm sure we'll have fun at the party. Everyone will be there.

7 Complete the sentences. Use *will* and *going to*.

1 I / do my homework now. Perhaps I / phone my friends later.
   I'm going to do my homework now. Perhaps I'll phone my friends later.
2 We / play football on Saturday. We hope we / win.
3 He / get a bike for his birthday. Maybe it / be red.
4 Lola is ill. She / not go school today. Perhaps she / feel better tomorrow.
5 We / watch a DVD tonight. I hope it / be a scary film.
6 I / not go to the sports event. Maybe people / not notice.

Vocabulary   Verb + preposition

1))) 3.5 **Look at the phrases. Check the meaning in a dictionary. Listen and repeat.**

agree with	apologise for	argue with	believe in
care about	decide on	disapprove of	hope for
insist on	know about	protest against	worry about

> **Word list** page 111   **Workbook** page 110

2 Match the beginnings (1–7) to the endings (a–g) of the sentences.

1 She apologised *a*
2 We have to decide on *a*
3 I don't believe
4 Everyone hopes
5 Do you know
6 On his birthday Karl insisted
7 I don't want to argue

a for her bad behaviour.
b in charity. People should help themselves.
c with you. Can't we just be friends?
d for a better world.
e about the party on Saturday night?
f on getting a pet snake.
g topic for our school project.

3 Complete the text. Use the correct prepositions.

Walk around the Barrio Gótico in Barcelona and you'll see strange marks on the road. They say 'city residents' on one side and 'tourists' on the other. People are worried [1] *about* the number of tourists in the city and the marks show people are protesting [2] .... this.
Many people agree [3] .... the protest. 'Sometimes I can't cross the street because there are so many tourists,' says Nuria Cugat. 'They're noisy and rude. They don't care [4] .... our city.'
Julio Sanchez disapproves [5] .... the protest. 'I can't argue [6] .... Nuria about the noise, especially at night, but we need tourism.'

4 In pairs, ask and answer.

1 How often do you argue with your parents?
2 Do you usually agree with your friends/ brothers/sisters?
3 Do you worry about exams?
4 What things do you care about?
5 Have you ever protested against something? What was it?

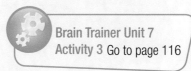

Brain Trainer Unit 7
Activity 3 Go to page 116

Chatroom Persuading

Speaking and Listening

1 **Look at the photo. Answer the questions.**

    1 Where are the teenagers?
    2 What do you think they are doing?
    3 What do the slogans on their T-shirts say?
    4 What do you think Ella is saying to Ruby?

2 **3.6 Listen and read the conversation. Check your answers.**

3 **3.6 Listen and read again. Answer the questions.**

    1 Why are they protesting?

    The local council is going to close down the library.

    2 What does Ella want Ruby to do?
    3 Why can't Ruby join them?
    4 What does Ella say they've got?
    5 What does Ash say she can do?
    6 Why does Tom think the demonstration is important?

4 **Act out the conversation in groups of four.**

Ruby	Hi, guys. What are you doing here?
Tom	We're protesting.
Ruby	What are you protesting against?
Ash	The local council is going to close down the library. They say that people don't use it, but that's rubbish!
Ella	Will you sign our petition? If you sign it, you'll help to keep the library open.
Ruby	I suppose so.
Tom	Hey, why don't you join us?
Ruby	Sorry, I can't. I've got homework to do.
Ella	Come on, Ruby. It'll be fun. Look, we've got T-shirts with slogans.
Ash	And you can hold my placard. It's better than doing homework.
Ruby	I don't know.
Tom	But it's important. We all use the library and we care about what happens to it. If we don't protest, they <u>will</u> close it. I'm **sure** you don't want that to happen.
Ruby	OK, I'll do it. You win! Where's my T-shirt?!

Say it in your language …

That's rubbish!
I suppose so.
You win!

5 Look back at the conversation. Who says what?

1 Come on Ruby. *Ella*
2 It'll be fun.
3 It's better than doing homework.
4 I'm sure you don't want that to happen.

6 Read the phrases for persuading and responding.

Persuading	Responding
Come on. It'll be fun.	I don't know.
It's better than … + *ing*.	OK, I'll do it.
I'm sure you …	

7 🔊 **3.7** Listen to the conversation. What is Ruby persuading Tom to do? Act out the conversation.

Tom This is ¹ difficult!
Ruby Come on, Tom. It'll be fun.
Tom I don't know. This is the first time I've ² been on a skateboard. I'm going to ³ fall over!
Ruby No, you're not. I'm sure you'll be fine.
Tom OK, you win! Hey, this is easier than I thought.
Ruby Yes – and it's better than ⁴ playing football!

8 Work in pairs. Replace the words in purple in Exercise 7. Use these words and/or your own ideas. Act out the conversations.

This is boring!

Come on …

1 hard / dangerous / tiring

2 played the guitar / ridden a scooter / trained for a marathon

3 hurt my fingers / fall off / stop after 5 km

4 listening to music / playing a computer game / going for a bike ride

Grammar First conditional

if + Present simple, *will* + infinitive
If we don't protest, they will close the library.

will ('ll) + verb > *if* + Present simple
They will close the library if we don't protest.

▶ **Grammar reference** Workbook page 98

1 Study the grammar table. Choose the correct options to complete the rules.

1 We use the First conditional to talk about *possible / impossible* situations.
2 The Present simple after *if* talks about events in *the future / the present*.

2 Complete the sentences.

1 If I *buy* (buy) a new T-shirt, it *won't have* (not have) a slogan.
2 You …. (not pass) your exam if you …. (not revise).
3 If you …. (care about) your friend, you …. (help) him.
4 He …. (laugh) if you …. (tell) him a joke.
5 If we …. (have) a school sit-in, there …. (be) trouble!
6 She …. (have) fun if she …. (go) to the fundraising event.
7 If they …. (be) worried about the library, they …. (sign) the petition.
8 I …. (get) angry if you …. (argue) with me.

3 Complete the sentences in your own words.

1 If I save some money, …. .
2 If I have some time tonight, …. .
3 If it's sunny this weekend, …. .
4 If I have a birthday party, …. .
5 If we go on holiday, …. .

4 In pairs, ask and answer about your sentences in Exercise 3.

What will you do if you save some money?

I'll buy a new watch.

83

Reading

1 **Look at the title of the magazine article and the photos. What do you think the article is going to be about?**

Eco World

Do something different ...

You don't have to go on a march or sign a petition to make a difference and change things. This week in *Eco World* magazine, we look at other ways you can protest.

2 🔊 3.8 **Read the article. Copy the table and match the organisations to the things they are protesting against.**

cars   ~~climate change~~
dangerous roads environmental damage
global warming pollution in cities

350.org	CM bike rides
climate change	

3 **Read the article again. Answer the questions.**

1 How does 350.org believe you can make people listen?

If you do something different, more people will listen.

2 What was unusual about how you could see the art exhibition?
3 What did Jorge Rodriguez-Gerada do?
4 How can people see his picture?
5 Where was the first CM bike ride?
6 Why did cars stop for the bikes?
7 How many cyclists are usually on a ride now?
8 How have the CM protests made a difference?

350.org

350.org is an organisation that protests against climate change. They believe that if you do something different, more people will listen. In 2010, it organised the world's biggest art exhibition called eARTh. People in sixteen different countries made huge pictures on the ground outside. You could only see the pictures from satellites in space. In the Delta del Ebro in Spain, an artist called Jorge Rodriguez-Gerada created a picture of a little girl called Galla. Galla was worried about global warming and the picture is about what might happen to the river Ebro. Hundreds of volunteers helped Jorge make it and thousands of people have seen it on Google Earth™.

Critical Mass bike rides

On a Friday evening in September 1992, sixty cyclists met in San Francisco and went on a bike ride. There was a lot of traffic on the roads, but there were a lot of bikes, too, so cars stopped for them. This was the world's first Critical Mass bike ride. Cyclists on the ride were protesting against cars and pollution. They wanted safer roads for cyclists. Today over 200 cities have CM bike rides. Rides are on the last Friday of every month and there are often more than 1,000 cyclists. The protests have made a difference and many cities now have bicycle lanes and 'car free' days. This year the biggest bike ride will be on Earth Day in Budapest. 'There are going to be 80,000 people on 80,000 bikes!' says one cyclist. Imagine that!

Key Words

organisation	climate change
traffic	pollution
bicycle lanes	

4 **Think about protests that have happened in your country. Choose one example.**

1 What was the problem?
2 How did people protest? What did they do?
3 What happened after the protest? Did it make a difference?

Listening

1 🔊 3.9 **Listen to the interview about a charity. Answer the questions.**

1 Who does Link Romania help?
2 What does it do?

🔊 **Listening Bank Unit 7** page 120

Writing A formal letter

1 **Read the Writing File.**

> **Writing File** Letter writing
>
> When you write a letter or email to a magazine, you can use these phrases.
>
> - **Opening**
>   *Dear (+ name of person or magazine)*
>
> - **Say why you are writing**
>   *I am writing to comment on …*
>
> - **Closing**
>   *Kind regards (+ your name)*
>   *Best wishes (+ your name)*

2 **Read the letter. Match the parts (1–5) to (a–e).**

a reason for writing
b opening the letter *1*
c closing the letter
d What action can we take?
e What is the problem?

Eco World Letters page

1 *Dear Eco World*

2 *I am writing to comment on your article about cycling to school in this week's magazine. In the article you say not many kids cycle. I think that this is because there are not enough bicycle lanes. Kids don't feel safe on a bike, so most of them go to school by car (including me!).*

3 *If people don't cycle, there will be more traffic on the road and more pollution. This is bad news for the environment.*

4 *How can we encourage people to get on their bikes? The solution is clear: we need more bicycle lanes. If we sign a petition asking for bicycle lanes, maybe the local council will listen. If there are more lanes, more kids will cycle to school!*

5 *Kind regards*

Samantha Kippel

3 **Read the letter again. Answer the questions.**

1 Why is Samantha writing to *Eco World*?
She wants to comment on an article about cycling.

2 Why don't children cycle to school?
3 How does Samantha go to school?
4 Why is this bad news for the environment?
5 What does Samantha suggest?

4 **Match these problems (1–4) to the headlines (a–b) from *Eco World*.**

1 There won't be a place for kids to play.
2 We won't have a place to study.
3 There won't be a place for people to read.
4 We won't have a place for people to walk.

a **Park is going, car park is coming!**

Our local park is going to become a car park. Lots of people use the park – there's a children's play area and a café there.

b **Library is going to close**

The local council has decided to close our library. They say that the library is too expensive and not many people use it.

5 **Choose one article from Exercise 4. Make notes about the problems. Try to think of a solution.**

6 **Write a letter to *Eco World* about the article you chose in Exercise 5. Use 'My formal letter' and your notes from Exercise 5.**

> **My formal letter**
>
> **1 Opening**
>   *Dear Eco World*
> **2 Reason for writing and the problem**
>   *I am writing to comment on the article about …*
>   *In the article you say that …*
> **3 Action**
>   *How can we save our …?*
> **4 Closing**
>   *Kind regards/Best wishes*

Remember!
- Use phrases from the Writing File.
- Use the vocabulary in this unit.
- Check your grammar, spelling and punctuation.

Refresh Your Memory!

Grammar Review

1 Complete the sentences. Use *going to* and these verbs.

~~do~~	have	not go	not watch	send	wear

1 I *'m going to do* some revision tonight. I've got an exam tomorrow!
2 We .... the concert this weekend. We haven't got tickets.
3 .... they .... a picnic? It's a lovely sunny day.
4 He .... the football match. He hates football!
5 .... she .... invitations to the party?
6 It's cold outside. .... you .... a coat?

2 Complete the sentences. Use *will* or *going to* and the verbs.

1 Perhaps I*'ll wear* (wear) a dress to the party. I don't know.
2 Brett is wearing his cycle helmet. He .... (ride) his bike.
3 Let's go on a boat ride. Maybe we .... (see) a dolphin.
4 She .... (go) skiing this winter. She's booked a hotel in the Alps.
5 Maybe it .... (be) sunny later, then we can go to the beach.
6 I .... (watch) my favourite TV programme tonight. It starts at 7 p.m.

3 Match the beginnings (1–6) to the endings (a–f) of the sentences.

1 If we sign the petition, *f*
2 If she says 'sorry',
3 If they go shopping,
4 He won't be happy
5 You'll get a nice tan

a will you be friends again?
b if his team loses.
c they'll buy some new clothes.
d if you lie in the sun.
e we'll make a difference.

Vocabulary Review

4 Choose the best options.

1 There's a *march / sit-in* today. It starts in the city centre and ends at the park.
2 I gave £5 to UNICEF today. Have you ever made a *donation / collection* to a charity?
3 It was a successful *petition / fundraising event*. We made £5,000 for the hospital!
4 I like the *slogan / banner* on your T-shirt. 'Save the Planet' is cool!
5 The *fundraising event / demonstration* went really well. People were protesting against the government.
6 The WWF is *a charity / a collection* that helps animals.
7 Protestors were carrying *placards / slogans* with *placards / slogans* on them. They said 'Save our jobs!'

5 Complete the sentences with these words.

agree	apologised	argue	care
insists	know	~~protested~~	worried

1 Lots of people *protested* against the new road.
2 I .... for forgetting my homework.
3 Do you .... about animals in danger?
4 I'm not .... about my exams. I know I'll do OK.
5 Do you .... with me?
6 Do you .... about the party this weekend? It's at Helga's.
7 I never .... with my girlfriend.
8 Our teacher always .... on silence in class.

Speaking Review

6 🔊 **3.10** **Put the conversation in the correct order. Then listen and check.**

Girl I don't want to make these banners. I'm bored. *1*
Boy No, it won't. I'm sure we'll finish them quickly.
Girl OK, you win! It's better than doing it on my own.
Boy Come on, I'll help you. It'll be fun.
Girl I don't know. There's a lot of work to do. It's going to take a long time!

Dictation

7 🔊 **3.11** **Listen and write in your notebook.**

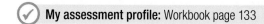 **My assessment profile:** Workbook page 133

Global Citizenship File

FAIRTRADE: CHOCOLATE +

Fairtrade™

1 What is it?

Shopping connects us with millions of people across the world. These people work on farms and in factories and they make the things we buy. Many of them come from developing countries and big companies don't pay them much money. Fairtrade companies give people a fair price for the work they do. They help people look after their families and buy the things they need. They also make sure that people work in safe conditions. Sometimes you pay a little bit more for Fairtrade products, but if we pay a bit more, people in other countries will have better lives.

Fairtrade fact file: chocolate

2 ....

Chocolate comes from cocoa beans on cocoa trees. Cocoa trees grow in countries with a tropical climate. Cameroon, Cote d'Ivoire and Ghana all grow cocoa beans. Countries like these are often very poor.

3 ....

Cocoa farmers. Many farmers earn less than fifty cents a day. They grow their own food, but it's hard for them to pay for other things like medicine and clothes.

4 ....

Farmers get more money for their work, so they can buy medicine and send their children to school. Some villages now have access to clean water, too. Farmers also get help and advice about farming. They learn new skills, so they become better farmers.

5 ....

- Find Fairtrade chocolate at your local supermarket, then vote with your wallet and buy it!
- Encourage your friends and family to do the same.
- Make your school Fairtrade-friendly. Design a poster, or start a petition.
- Ask for Fairtrade products (not just chocolate!). There are more than 3,000 Fairtrade products to choose from!

Key Words

farms	factories
developing country	fair price
tropical climate	vote

Reading

1 **Read the article quickly. Match the headings (A–E) to the paragraphs (1–5).**

A What is it? *1*
B Who makes it?
C How does Fairtrade help?
D What can we do?
E Where is it from?

2 🔊 3.12 **Read the article again. Are these sentences true (T) or false (F)?**

1 Big companies pay people more money than Fairtrade companies. *F*
2 Fairtrade products are sometimes more expensive than normal products.
3 Countries that grow cocoa beans are usually rich.
4 Cocoa farmers have to pay for their food.
5 Fairtrade helps farmers improve their work.
6 There aren't many Fairtrade products.

My Global Citizenship File

3 **Choose another Fairtrade product and make notes about it. Think about:**
- where it is from
- who grows or makes it
- how Fairtrade helps
- what we can do to help

4 **Write a Fairtrade fact file about your product. Add photos or pictures. Use your notes from Exercise 3 to help you.**

8 Danger And Risk

Grammar	Second conditional; Relative pronouns
Vocabulary	Extreme adjectives; Illness and injury
Speaking	Talking about health
Writing	An application form

Vocabulary Extreme adjectives

1 🔊 **3.13** **Listen and repeat. Then match the normal adjectives (1–10) to the extreme adjectives in the box. Check your answers in a dictionary.**

| awful | boiling | ~~brilliant~~ | exhausted | freezing |
| furious | huge | terrifying | thrilled | tiny |

1 good *brilliant*   **6** big
2 small   **7** bad
3 hot   **8** pleased
4 cold   **9** angry
5 scary   **10** tired

Word list page 111   **Workbook** page 111

2 **Match the comments (1–3) to the photos (a–c).**
1 It's huge and he's tiny. It looks freezing cold.
2 It's a brilliant picture. It looks terrifying.
3 It's an awful place. I think she's exhausted.

3 🔊 **3.14** **Complete the conversations with extreme adjectives. Listen and check, then practise with a partner.**
A Was the film really good?
B It was ¹ *brilliant*.

A Are you very tired?
B Yes, it's late. I'm ² .... .

A Brr! It's really cold in here.
B You're right. It's ³ .... . Have you got a jumper?

A Is he really pleased with his exam results?
B He's ⁴ .... . He did really well.

A Was your mum very angry that you stayed out late?
B Yes, she was. She was ⁵ ....!

4 **What about you? In pairs, ask and answer.**
Have you ever …
• watched a terrifying film?
• had brilliant exam results?
• picked up a huge spider?

Brain Trainer Unit 8
Activity 2 Go to page 116

Reading

1 You are going to read about an unusual job. Before you read, look at the photo and answer the questions.

    1 What type of job do you think it is?
    2 How do you think the person feels?
    3 Why do you think he/she does it?

2 Read the interview quickly and check your answers.

3 Work in pairs. Find these numbers in the interview. What do they refer to?

- 80
- 1,000,000
- 8
- 100

4))) **3.15** Read the interview again. Are these sentences true (T) or false (F)?

    1 In today's films, computers create most of the stunts. *F*
    2 Stunts can be very expensive.
    3 Naomi doesn't earn much money.
    4 She was tired after her first job.
    5 She has had a lot of accidents.
    6 She thinks a police officer's job is more dangerous.

5 In pairs, ask and answer.

    1 Do you think Naomi's job is dangerous?
    2 Can you think of other dangerous jobs?
    3 Do you know anyone who does a dangerous job?
    4 Would you like to be a stuntman or woman? Why?/Why not?

Interview: Naomi Daniels

← → C ⌂

Interview:
Naomi Daniels

Today's action films are often thrilling adventures with amazing stunts. Computers create some of these stunts, but stuntmen and women do most of them. In some action films there are more than eighty stuntmen and women and one stunt can cost over a million dollars! It's an exciting job, but what about the risks? We interviewed stuntwoman Naomi Daniels.

Naomi, why are you a stuntwoman?
Because it's a brilliant job! I earn a lot of money, I travel around the world, I meet famous people and I never do the same thing twice. If I wasn't a stuntwoman, I'd do extreme sports. But stunts are more fun!

Can you remember your first job?
Yes, I can. It was a car race in the desert. It was boiling hot and it took eight hours to film. At the end of the day I was exhausted.

Do you ever worry about the risks?
Sometimes, but I practise a lot and I'm very careful. I don't usually have accidents, but last year I hurt my leg. I was furious because it was an easy stunt – a jump from a hundred-metre bridge!

If I were you, I'd be really frightened!
Well, if I was scared, I wouldn't be a stuntwoman.

Would you be happier if you had a normal job?
No, I wouldn't. If I had a normal job, I'd be bored. And I don't think my job is dangerous. When I see police officers or firefighters, then I think, 'Wow, that's dangerous.'

Grammar   Second conditional

if + Past simple, would ('d) + verb would ('d) + verb > if + Past simple
Affirmative
If I had a normal job, I'd be bored.
Negative
If I wasn't a stuntwoman, I'd do extreme sports. If I was scared, I wouldn't be a stuntwoman.
Questions and short answers
Would you be happier if you had a normal job? Yes, I would./No, I wouldn't.

Watch Out!

If I were you, I'd be terrified.
= If I ~~was~~ you, I'd be terrified.

Grammar reference Workbook page 100

1 Study the grammar table. Choose the correct options to complete the rules.

1 We use the Second conditional to talk about *probable / improbable* situations or *real / unreal* events.
2 The Past simple after *if* talks about events now or *in the future / in the past*.

2 Choose the correct options.

1 If I could choose any job, I *would be / will be* a firefighter.
2 If I *forgot / forget* my friend's birthday, I would feel embarrassed.
3 He would be furious if you *copied / copy* his homework.
4 If we learned another language, we *studied / would study* Chinese.
5 I would wear a big coat if it *is / was* freezing outside.
6 If she went to bed late, she *is feeling / would feel* exhausted.
7 It *will be / would be* awful if they had an accident.
8 If I could meet anyone in the world, it *would be / will be* Justin Bieber.

3 Complete the text with the correct form of the verbs.

If you ¹ *had* (have) tickets for a huge, terrifying rollercoaster ride, what ².... (you/do)? 'I'd go on it,' says Joel Alvaro. 'If I ³.... (can) ride rollercoasters all day, I ⁴.... (do) it,' he adds, 'but I have to go to work.' Joel is a teacher – he also loves funfairs. 'If I ⁵.... (live) in Orlando in America, I ⁶.... (feel) thrilled,' he says. Orlando has got the most rollercoaster rides in the world! If he ⁷.... (be) in Orlando, he ⁸.... (visit) Disney World every day and he'd ride Space Mountain. But he doesn't. His girlfriend thinks he's crazy. 'Rollercoasters are fun, but if I ⁹.... (go) on them all the time, I ¹⁰.... (get) bored and feel sick!' she says.

4 Look at these situations. Make questions.

1 you / see / a film star
   What would you do if you saw a film star?
2 you / find / 50 euros in the street
3 you / lose / your school bag
4 your friend / break / your mobile phone
5 your parents / be / furious with you
6 your friend / steal / from a shop

5 In pairs, ask and answer the questions in Exercise 4.

What would you do if you saw a film star?

I'd ask them for their autograph.

Vocabulary Illness and injury

1 🔊 **3.16** Match the pictures (1–12) to these words and phrases. Then listen, check and repeat.

a burn	a cold	a cough
a cut	a headache	a rash *1*
a sore throat	a sprained ankle	a stomachache
a temperature	backache	toothache

Word list page 111 **Workbook** page 111

2 What's wrong with these people?

1 My head hurts. I'm going to take an aspirin.
a headache
2 I was walking down the stairs when I fell. Now I can't walk.
3 I can't eat anything. There's something wrong with my tooth.
4 I can't lift that heavy box. There's something wrong with my back.
5 My head feels hot, but I feel cold. I need a blanket.
6 I've eaten too much. I feel ill.
7 I had an accident. I hurt my finger with a knife.

3 Complete the sentences with the words in Exercise 1.

1 He dropped boiling water on his hand and now he's got a really bad *burn*.
2 My nose is red and I don't feel very well. I think I've got a .... .
3 I wish my .... would go away. It wakes me up at night.
4 I've got a .... . It hurts when I eat or drink.
5 She's got a .... on her leg – it looks really deep.

Pronunciation *gh*

4a 🔊 **3.17** Listen and repeat. How do we pronounce *gh* in these words?

brought	cough	eight	enough
high	laugh	rough	thought

b 🔊 **3.18** Copy the table and put the words in Exercise 4a in the correct column. Then listen and check.

/f/	silent
cough	*brought*

c 🔊 **3.19** Listen and repeat. Be careful with the *gh* sound.

1 It's eight o'clock.
2 Have you had enough to drink?
3 I brought some medicine for your cough.
4 Don't laugh. I thought you were ill!

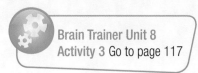

Brain Trainer Unit 8
Activity 3 Go to page 117

Chatroom · Talking about health

Speaking and Listening

1 **Look at the photo. Answer the questions.**

  1 Where are Tom and Ruby?
  2 What's wrong with Ruby?
  3 What has Tom done?

2))) **3.20** **Listen and read the conversation. Check your answers.**

3))) **3.20** **Listen and read again. Answer the questions.**

  1 How did Ruby hurt herself?
    She fell over a cat.

  2 Where was the woman?
  3 What does Tom do at the O$_2$ arena?
  4 How did Tom hurt himself?
  5 What does he think is wrong?
  6 Why does Ruby feel sorry for Tom?

4 **Act out the conversation in pairs.**

Tom Hi, Ruby. What's the matter?
Ruby Oh, I've hurt my arm.
Tom How did you do that?
Ruby Well, I fell over a cat which ran out from under a car.
Tom That's awful!
Ruby The cat was OK, but my arm wasn't. The woman who was in the car brought me here. Oww!
Tom Are you all right?
Ruby Don't worry, I'm fine. So why are you here?
Tom I had a silly accident at the O$_2$ arena.
Ruby The what?
Tom The O$_2$ arena, you know … it's the place where I play football.
Ruby So what happened?
Tom I was trying to score a goal when I fell over the ball.
Ruby That's funny, except your leg looks terrible. How does it feel?
Tom Not too good. I think I've got a sprained ankle. And we lost the game.
Ruby Poor you!

Say it in your language …
That's awful!
Poor you!

5 Look back at the conversation. Complete the sentences.

1 *What's* the matter?
2 I've .... my arm.
3 Are you .... ?
4 I'm .... .
5 .... does it feel?

6 Read the phrases for asking and talking about health.

Asking about health	Responding
What's the matter?	I've got a headache/ a sprained ankle/ toothache, etc.
Are you all right?	I'm fine, thanks.
How does it feel?	Not too good.
How do you feel?	A bit better, thanks.

7 🔊 3.21 Listen to the conversations. What's wrong with Tom and Ella? Act out the conversations in pairs.

Ash Hi, Tom. You look awful! What's the matter?
Tom Atchoo. I've got ¹ a cold.
Ash Poor you! How do you feel?
Tom Not too good.

Ella I feel awful. I've got ¹ a headache.
Ash Can I get you anything?
Ella No, I'm fine, thanks. … OK, maybe ² a hot drink.
Ash You should ³ have a rest, too.

8 Work in pairs. Replace the words in purple in Exercise 7. Use these words and phrases and/ or your own ideas. Act out the conversations.

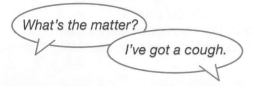

1 backache / a sprained ankle / toothache

2 a hot water bottle / some ice / some medicine

3 go to the doctor's / take an aspirin / go to the dentist's

Grammar   Relative pronouns

It's the place where I play football.
She's the woman who was in the car.
That's the cat which was under a car.

▸ Grammar reference Workbook page 100

1 Study the grammar table. Complete the rule with *who, which* or *where*.

We use relative pronouns to talk about places (....), people (....) and things (....).

2 Choose the correct options.

1 I don't like stories *who / which* make me cry.
2 That's the cinema *which / where* I saw that brilliant film.
3 This is the bag *which / who* is very heavy. The others are OK.
4 There's the beach *where / which* we went swimming last year.
5 She's the girl *who / which* is good at football.
6 That's the TV show *which / who* is all about doctors.

3 Complete the sentences with *who, which* or *where*.

1 I hate films *which* are scary.
2 He's someone .... is very kind.
3 It's the place .... we went for Tom's birthday.
4 Those are the jeans .... were very expensive.
5 That's the pizzeria .... I go with my family.
6 I like mobile phones .... are very small.
7 She's the teacher .... is always late.
8 These are the people .... are coming to the party.

4 Complete the conversation with *who, which* or *where*.

A There's the boy ¹ *who* won the competition.
B Oh yes? Where was that?
A It was at the skatepark ² .... is near the beach.
B I don't know it.
A Well, it's the place ³ .... I go at the weekend.
B Is it good?
A Yes, it's got a café ⁴ .... you can meet friends. Look! He's walking this way.
B Is he the tall one?
A No, he's wearing a black T-shirt ⁵ .... has got a cool slogan.
B Ah yes, there's a girl ⁶ .... is talking to him. She's holding a mobile phone ⁷ .... has got a pink cover.
A That's right. Hmm, do you think she's his girlfriend?

Reading

1 **Look at the photo. Answer the questions.**

   1 What's happening in the photo?
   2 How does the girl feel? How would you feel?
   3 Why do you think people take risks?

This week's
**big
question:**

**Why
are
people
risk-
takers?**

1 It's all about adrenalin

Recently there have been amazing
teenagers in the news. Laura
Dekker has sailed around the
world, Parker Liautaud has skied
⁵ to the North Pole and Amelia
Hempleman-Adams has skied to
the South Pole. These teenagers
are all natural risk-takers, but why
do they do it? We looked at some
¹⁰ popular explanations.

Some scientists believe that
risk-takers' bodies don't react
to danger like most people's
¹⁵ bodies. When we are in danger,
our bodies make a chemical
called adrenalin. It stimulates
our brain and makes us ready
to fight or run away. Risk-
²⁰ takers' bodies don't make
adrenalin easily, so they take
more risks to feel 'alive'.

2 Little old women don't
go snowboarding

²⁵ Studies have shown that tall
people take more risks than
small people, women are more
careful than men and older
people take fewer risks than

³⁰ younger people. Tall people are
often confident and confident
people are not easily scared.
Scientists also think that men
are more natural risk-takers
³⁵ than women and that age and
experience make people more
cautious … or really boring!

3 Be careful what you watch

Recent research asked these
⁴⁰ questions, too. If you played
a computer game about risk-
taking, would that make you
take risks in real life? And if
your parents or friends took
⁴⁵ risks, would you take them,
too? It seems the answer to
both questions is yes!

And finally … some researchers
say that risk-takers are
⁵⁰ frequently bored – they often
change jobs and they don't
have long relationships. But
some people say they are
happier – what do you think?

Key Words

risk-taker   scientist   react
stimulate   research

2 **Read the magazine article and check your
answers to Exercise 1.**

3 **Find these words in the article. In pairs, try to
explain what they mean. Look them up in a
dictionary to check.**

   1 chemical (line 16)
   2 confident (line 31)
   3 cautious (line 37)
   4 frequently (line 50)

4 🔊 **3.22** **Read the article again. Answer
the questions.**

   1 What do the teenagers in the introduction
have in common?
   They are all risk-takers.
   2 What does adrenalin do to our brains?
   3 Why do risk-takers take risks?
   4 Why do tall people take more risks?
   5 What happens when we get older?
   6 How do risk-takers often feel?

5 **In groups, discuss these questions.**

   1 Are you tall, young and healthy?
   2 Do you ever feel scared?
   3 Do you love computer games?
   4 Do you think you are a risk-taker? Why?/Why not?

Listening

1 🔊 **3.23** **Listen to two people talking about a
TV show. Answer the questions.**

   1 What's the show called?
   2 Name two things the teenagers have to do.
   3 What's the prize?

🔊 **Listening Bank Unit 8** page 120

Writing   An application form

1   Read the Writing File.

> ### Writing File   Completing an application form
>
> - Read the questions: do you have to write information or choose an answer?
> - If you have to write information, what kind of information is it? (name, date, number?)
> - If you have to choose an answer, read all the answers first.
> - Complete the form.
> - Check what you have written.

2   Read the application form for the *Spider Island* TV show. Complete the questions with these words.

how (x2)	how many	what	where	why

Send your application form to:
Spider Island
Roundhouse Road
London
NQ4 9TU

Spider Island
Application Form

Name *Casey MacDonald*   Age *14*

1 .... adventurous are you? (5 = very, 1 = not at all)
  1 ☐   2 ☐   3 ☐   4 ☑   5 ☐

2 .... of the activities have you done? (tick the boxes)
camping ☑ climbing ☑ sailing ☐ fishing ☑ cooking ☐

3 If you could visit <u>one</u> of these places, ... would you go?
Tick the box. Say why.
the jungle ☐   a desert island ☐   Disney World ☑
I'd like to go to Disney World because I love
rollercoasters and it would be really exciting.

4 .... would your best friend describe you? Circle four words.
(adventurous)   nervous   (funny)   serious
(happy)   moody   (friendly)   shy

5 .... are you scared of?
I'm terrified of losing.

6 .... do you want to go to Spider Island?
Because I love trying new things. I also
want to be on TV!

3   Match the question words (1–6) to the answers (a–f). What type of information do the answers give (e.g. a number, a date, a place, a person, a reason, a thing)?

1 What *f*
2 Who
3 How many
4 Where
5 When
6 Why

a Because it's my birthday.
b On Friday 12th June.
c My friends.
d At the pizzeria.
e Twelve.
f A party.

4   Read the application form again. Answer the questions.

1 Which activities has Casey never tried?
   Sailing and cooking
2 Where would he like to go?
3 Is he a confident person?
4 What is he worried about?
5 Why does he want to be on the show?

5   Copy and complete the application form for you.

> ### Remember!
> - First, read the questions: do you have to circle or tick an answer or write information?
> - If you have to write information, what kind of information is it?
> - If you have to choose an answer, read all the answers first.
> - Complete the form.
> - Check what you have written in the form carefully.
> - Use the vocabulary in this unit.
> - Check your grammar, spelling and punctuation.

Refresh Your Memory!

Grammar Review

1 **Complete the sentences. Use the Second conditional.**

1 If she *didn't have* (not have) homework, she'd watch the action film.
2 .... (he/travel) abroad if he had more time?
3 They .... (climb) the mountain if it stopped snowing.
4 If he was frightened of spiders, he .... (not pick) them up.
5 If you .... (be) famous, would you be my friend?
6 What .... (you/do) if you lost your mobile phone?
7 If people .... (not take) risks, would they be happier?

2 **Read the sentences. Are the explanations (a and b) true (T) or false (F)?**

1 If I could sing, I'd be a pop star.
  a I can sing very well. *F*
  b I can't sing at all. *T*
2 If he went on the rollercoaster ride, he'd enjoy it.
  a He probably won't go on the ride.
  b He's going to go on the ride.
3 If she worked hard, she'd be top of the class.
  a She works hard.
  b She doesn't work hard.
4 If they were good at football, they'd be in the school team.
  a They are in the school team.
  b They aren't in the school team.
5 I'd be furious if you broke my MP3 player.
  a You probably won't break it.
  b The MP3 player doesn't work.
6 If I could meet anyone in the world, I'd choose Lady Gaga.
  a You'll probably never meet her.
  b You're going to meet her next week.

3 **Choose the correct options.**

1 A nurse is a person *who / which* looks after people.
2 The cinema is a place *which / where* we can watch films.
3 There's the girl *which / who* was late for class.
4 Cycling is a sport *who / which* is good for you.
5 Isn't that the hotel *which / where* we stayed?
6 The café *where / who* I meet my friends is on North Street.
7 I like those trainers – the ones *who / which* are 29 euros.
8 The boy *which / who* invited me to the party is called Tom.

Vocabulary Review

4 **Replace the words in bold with extreme adjectives.**

awful	boiling	~~exhausted~~	freezing
huge	terrifying	thrilled	tiny

1 I've done a lot of homework today. I'm **really tired**! *exhausted*
2 The burger was **very big**, but he ate it all.
3 Be careful! The water is **really hot**!
4 The bird was **very small**. I held it in my hand.
5 Jody was **very pleased** with her birthday present.
6 I didn't enjoy the party. The music was **very bad**.
7 It's **really cold** outside. It's started to snow.
8 The horror film was **very scary**.

5 **Match the illnesses and injuries to the definitions.**

a cold	a headache	a sore throat
a sprained ankle	a stomachache	~~a temperature~~

1 This makes you feel hot and cold. *a temperature*
2 Your nose is sore.
3 This hurts when you walk.
4 Your stomach hurts.
5 Your throat hurts.
6 Your head and eyes hurt.

Speaking Review

6 🔊 **3.24** **Complete the conversation with these words. Then listen and check.**

~~all right~~	feel	get	got	how	too good

Girl You look awful! Are you ¹ *all right*?
Boy No, I'm not ² .... . I've ³ .... a stomachache.
Girl Poor you! Can I ⁴ .... you anything?
Boy Maybe a glass of water.
Girl Here you are. ⁵ .... do you ⁶ .... now?
Boy A bit better, thanks.

Dictation

7 🔊 **3.25** **Listen and write in your notebook.**

 My assessment profile: Workbook page 134

Real World Profiles

Crina 'Coco' Popescu's Profile

Age:
18 years old

Home country:
Romania

My favourite things …

climbing, cycling, running, swimming, travel, my family and friends

Reading

1 **Read Coco's profile. Correct the mistakes in this short text.**

Coco is a 16-year-old climber from Romania. As well as climbing, she loves cycling and skateboarding and she's also a good swimmer. She doesn't like travelling much, but she loves her family and friends.

2))) 3.26 **Read the magazine article. Answer the questions.**

1 What did Coco do when she was 16?

She climbed the highest mountain in Antarctica.

2 When did she start climbing?
3 How did she feel after climbing Dente del Gigante?
4 What does she do after school?
5 How is her free time different from her friends' free time?
6 Why did she give up on the Himalayan mountain?
7 How many world records has she broken?
8 Who has supported and encouraged her?

Coco loves climbing

In 2011, Crina 'Coco' Popescu climbed Mount Sidley, the highest mountain in Antarctica. The views from the top of the mountain were amazing, but the most amazing thing was Coco's age: she was only 16. Today Coco is 18 and she is also the youngest woman to climb the seven highest volcanoes in the world.

Coco started climbing when she was six years old. First, she climbed the mountains around her home town of Rasnov. Then, she started to climb bigger, more dangerous mountains. When she was 10, she climbed the huge Dente del Gigante mountain in the Alps. After the climb she was exhausted, but also excited … about her next challenge!

So how does she do it? Well, she works very hard. Coco trains every day after school. She also goes running, swimming and cycling. If she didn't train, she wouldn't be strong enough to go on expeditions. She doesn't have much time to watch movies, shop or go out with her friends.

Coco is a brilliant climber, but she doesn't take risks. In 2009, she was halfway up a mountain in the Himalayas when the weather suddenly changed. It was a dangerous situation and a terrifying experience. She gave up the expedition and went home. Coco was disappointed, but she learned from her ordeal. Today, with the help of her family and friends, she's broken six world records. 'I can't thank my parents enough for their support,' says Coco. 'I'm trying hard to make them proud.'

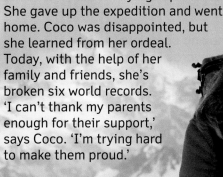

Class discussion

1 Are there any young record breakers like Coco in your country?
2 Are there any mountains in your country? Which is the highest mountain?
3 Which is the highest mountain in the world? Which country is it in?

(9) Inventions

Grammar	Present simple passive; Past simple passive
Vocabulary	Machine nouns and verbs; Word building
Speaking	Problems with machines
Writing	An opinion essay

Vocabulary Machine nouns and verbs

1 🔊 3.27 **Match the pictures (1–8) to these verbs. Then match the pictures (9–16) to these nouns. Then listen, check and repeat.**

Verbs:	attach	build	communicate *1*	invent
press	plug in	produce	switch on/off	

Nouns:	battery	button	cable	keyboard
remote control		socket	tube *9*	wheel

> **Word list** page 111   **Workbook** page 112

2 **Look at the machine and complete the instructions. Use the words in Exercise 1.**

MY MARVELLOUS ICE CREAM MAKER

¹ *Plug* in the cable to the nearest ² .... .
³ .... the red button to ⁴ .... the machine.
Put eggs, cream and sugar into the different ⁵ .... s.
Use the ⁶ .... to write the name of your favourite ice cream.
Turn the ⁷ .... or press the ⁸ .... s on the ⁹ .... control.
The machine will ¹⁰ .... some tasty ice cream.
Remember to ¹¹ .... the machine. Then enjoy!

3 **In pairs, take turns to describe one of these things. Use words from Exercise 1 and the phrases below.**

laptop	memory stick	mobile phone	torch
train	TV		

A *It's got a battery. Before you can use it, you have to switch it on. You can use it to produce light and to see in the dark.*

B *You can use it to ....*

Brain Trainer Unit 9
Activity 2 Go to page 117

Reading

1 Think of some famous inventors. What did they invent?

2 Read the magazine article quickly. Match the paragraphs (1–3) to the photos (a–c).

3 🔊 3.28 Read the article again. Are these sentences true (T) or false (F)?

1 Louis Braille could never see. *F*
2 His system of writing was a completely new idea.
3 Alexander Kendrick's invention can help people with injuries.
4 People should always have a mobile phone with them when they are caving.
5 Hibiki Kono's invention uses machines that many people have in their homes.
6 He uses his invention to climb the walls in his bedroom.

4 What do you think?

1 Which of the inventions in the photos is:
  a the cleverest?
  b the most useful?
  c the most fun?
  Say why.

> *I think the low-frequency radio is the cleverest invention. It's very difficult to build a radio and this radio can do things that other radios can't do.*

2 If you were an inventor, what would you invent?

> *I would invent a robot that could do all my homework for me!*

Teenage inventors

You don't have to be old with crazy white hair to invent something. Here are some of our favourite young inventors.

1 Louis Braille (1809–1852) was French. He became blind in an accident when he was only three years old. At the age of twelve, he learned about a system of writing with bumps in paper that you feel with your fingers. Louis liked this idea, but the writing was difficult to read. For the next three years, he worked on a similar but easier system. The result of his work was 'Braille' writing. The first book in Braille appeared in 1829 and Braille is still used by blind people today.

2 Sixteen-year-old Alexander Kendrick loves caving, but it's a very dangerous activity. When accidents happen underground, it's impossible to communicate with the outside world. Messages that are sent on traditional radios or mobile phones can't travel through rock. Alexander has built a special low-frequency radio that works 300 metres underground. It is made with plastic tubes and metal cable and messages are written on a keyboard. This clever machine might save a lot of lives in the future.

3 Gloves aren't usually used to climb walls, are they? Well, thirteen-year-old Hibiki Kono has invented special gloves! A small vacuum cleaner is attached to each glove. When the vacuum cleaners are switched on, the gloves can carry the weight of a large person on a wall or ceiling. But Hibiki isn't allowed to use the gloves in his bedroom. His mum thinks they're too dangerous.

Grammar   Present simple passive

Affirmative

It is made with plastic tubes.
They are made with plastic.

Negative

The machine isn't made with plastic.
Gloves aren't usually used to climb walls.

Questions and short answers

Is the machine made with plastic?
Yes, it is./No, it isn't.
Are the gloves used to climb walls?
Yes, they are./No, they aren't.

> **Grammar reference** Workbook page 102

1 **Study the grammar tables. Choose the correct options to complete the rules.**

> **1** We use the passive when we want to focus on *the action / the person or thing doing the action*.
> **2** We make the Present simple passive with the Present simple of *have / be* and the Past participle.

2 **Complete the sentences with the Present simple passive of the verbs.**

A lot happens around the world in one minute:
1 A hundred new cars *are produced* (produce).
2 The internet .... (use) by 64 million people.
3 Twelve million text messages .... (send).
4 10,000 songs .... (download) from the internet.
5 There is a lot of rubbish. In fact, 1.5 million kilograms of rubbish .... (throw away).

3 **Make sentences.**

1 our washing machine / run / every day
   Our washing machine is run every day.
2 the cables / not plug in / to the right sockets
3 My laptop isn't working. My homework / not save / on another computer!
4 batteries / not include

4 **Make questions. Then ask and answer in pairs.**

1 mobile phones / allow / in class?
   Are mobile phones allowed in class?
2 interactive whiteboards / use / at your school?
3 English / speak / all the time in your English class?
4 your TV / switch on / all evening?

Active and passive

Active

Blind people use Braille.
You write messages on a keyboard.

Passive

Braille is used by blind people.
Messages are written on a keyboard.

> **Grammar reference** Workbook page 102

5 **Study the grammar table. Choose the correct options to complete the rules.**

> **1** With an active verb, the person or thing that does the action goes *before / after* the verb.
> **2** With a passive verb, we *always / don't always* mention the person or thing that does the action.
> **3** With a passive verb, we introduce the person or thing that does the action with *by / for*.

6 **Change these active sentences into passive sentences. Don't include *by* + noun.**

1 People spend 75 billion euros on video games every year.
   75 billion euros *are spent on video games every year.*
2 People eat a lot of ice cream in summer.
   A lot of ice cream .... .
3 They don't sell those sweets in my town.
   Those sweets .... .
4 Teachers give too much homework to students.
   Too much homework .... .

7 **Change these active sentences into passive sentences. Include *by* + noun.**

1 A hairdresser usually cuts my hair.
   My hair *is usually cut by a hairdresser.*
2 The average teenager sends 875 text messages every month.
   875 text messages .... .
3 A Japanese company makes those mobile phones.
   Those mobile phones .... .
4 The sun warms the water in the pool.
   The water in the pool is .... .

Vocabulary   Word building

1 Do the quiz. Use your dictionary to help you if necessary.

2 🔊 3.29   Listen and check.

1 **What did Coco Chanel design?**
a *clothes*
b planes
c computers

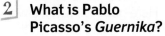
2 **What is Pablo Picasso's *Guernika*?**
a a film
b a book
c a painting

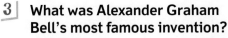
3 **What was Alexander Graham Bell's most famous invention?**
a the phone
b the radio
c the TV

4 **Who was the writer of *Romeo and Juliet*?**
a Charles Dickens
b William Shakespeare
c Agatha Christie

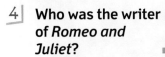
5 **Which company is a famous car producer?**
a Nokia
b Ikea
c Volvo

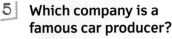
6 **What is the Taj Mahal?**
a a mountain
b a building
c a river

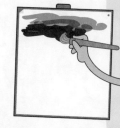

3 Copy and complete the table.

verb	noun 1: person	noun 2: result
build	builder	¹ *building*
²	designer	design
invent	inventor	³ ....
paint	painter	⁴ ....
produce	⁵	product
write	⁶	writing

Word list page 111   **Workbook** page 112

4 Complete the text with these words.

buildings	built	designs	inventor
~~painted~~	painter	paintings	produced

Leonardo da Vinci ¹ *painted* the *Mona Lisa*, one of the world's most famous ² .... and he ³ .... some beautiful works of art for the rooms of Italy's most important ⁴ .... . But he wasn't only a ⁵ .... . He was also the ⁶ .... of flying machines, musical instruments and hundreds of other things. Some experts have followed his ⁷ .... for a flying machine and have ⁸ .... one that can fly!

Pronunciation   /ɪ/ and /iː/

5a 🔊 3.30   **Listen and repeat.**

big	build	clean	email
internet	keyboard	silly	wheel

b 🔊 3.31   **Copy the table and put the words in Exercise 5a in the correct column. Then listen and check.**

/ɪ/	/iː/
big	*clean*

c 🔊 3.32   **Listen and repeat.**
1 The D on his keyboard's disappeared.
2 Switch on the big machine, please.
3 She's invented a brilliant new screen.

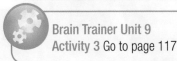
Brain Trainer Unit 9
Activity 3 Go to page 117

Chatroom Problems with machines

Speaking and Listening

1 Look at the photo. What do you think the girls are doing?

2 🔊 3.33 Listen and read the conversation. Check your answer.

3 🔊 3.33 Listen and read again. Complete the sentences.

   1 What did Ella make the robot from?
     A tin can.

   2 What did she find on the internet?
   3 What's the problem with the robot?
   4 How does Ella know that the battery is OK?
   5 Why didn't she see the red button before?
   5 How does the robot break?

4 Act out the conversation in pairs.

Ruby Is that your robot for the Science project? It's so cute! Was it made from a tin can?

Ella Yes, it was. But it doesn't work.

Ruby What's the problem?

Ella Well, the instructions weren't included in the box. I found some on the internet and I've done everything that they say, but the wheels don't move.

Ruby There might be something wrong with the battery. Have you checked it?

Ella Yes. It was only bought yesterday and it works OK in my torch.

Ruby Have you tried pressing that red button?

Ella No, I haven't – it was hidden under the robot's arm. Here goes … Yay! It's working!

Ruby Watch out, Ella! It's going to fall off the table! ***CRASH!***

Ella Oh no! It's broken. What am I going to do now?

👤 **Say it in your language …**
It's so cute!
Here goes.
Yay!

5 **Look back at the conversation. Complete the sentences.**

1 It doesn't *work.*
2 What's the .... ?
3 Have you .... it?
4 Have you .... pressing that red button?

6 **Read the phrases for talking about problems.**

Talking about problems with machines	
What's the problem?	It doesn't work. It's broken. The (wheels) don't (move).
Have you tried (pressing that button)?	No, I haven't.
There might be something wrong with the battery. Have you checked it?	

7 🔊 **3.34** **Listen to the conversation. What does Ash suggest? Act out the conversation in pairs.**

Ash Let's ¹ watch this DVD on your laptop.
Tom We can't. ² It doesn't work.
Ash What's the problem?
Tom ³ The laptop can't play it.
Ash There might be something wrong with ⁴ the DVD. Have you checked it?
Tom Yes. It works OK ⁵ in the DVD player.
Ash Have you tried ⁶ switching the laptop off and then on again?

8 **Work in pairs. Replace the words in purple in Exercise 7. Use these words and/or your own ideas. Act out the conversation.**

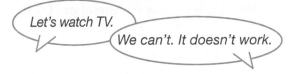

Let's watch TV.
We can't. It doesn't work.

1 download some songs to your MP3 player / send Ruby a text
2 my MP3 player / my mobile phone
3 nothing downloads to it / it can't send or get texts at the moment
4 the cable / the battery
5 with my dad's computer / and I charged it earlier
6 plugging it into the other socket / standing outside in the garden

Grammar   Past simple passive

Affirmative	Negative
It was made by Ella.	It wasn't made by Ella.
They were bought yesterday.	The instructions weren't included in the box.

Questions	
Was it made from a tin can? Yes, it was./No, it wasn't.	
Were the instructions included? Yes, they were./No, they weren't.	

▷ **Grammar reference** Workbook page 102

1 **Study the grammar table. Choose the correct option to complete the rule.**

We form the Past simple passive with the Past simple of *be / have* and the Past participle.

2 **Complete the text with the Past simple passive form of the verbs.**

The history of mobile phones
The first mobile phones were very big. They
¹ *were used* (use) on trains and planes in the 1920s. A mobile phone network ² .... (introduce) in Tokyo in 1979 and other cities soon followed. The first text message ³ .... (send) in Finland in 1993 and, later, mobile phones ⁴ .... (produce) that could take photos and use the internet. In 2010, more than five billion mobile phones ⁵ .... (own) by people around the world!

3 **Change these sentences into the passive. Only include *by* + noun if this is important.**

1 People in the USA invented the internet.
   The internet was invented in the USA.
2 Leonardo da Vinci didn't build the world's first plane.
3 My friend, Jack won the Science competition.
4 They didn't tell the students about the exams.
5 My dad designed our house.

4 **Make questions in the Past simple passive. Then ask and answer.**

1 your favourite photos / take / on a mobile phone?
   Were your favourite photos taken on a mobile phone?
2 your favourite book / write / a long time ago?
3 your favourite films / make / in your country?
4 your class / give / a lot of homework last week?

Reading

1 Look at the photos (a–d). Put the inventions in the order that they were invented.

A **book** for all time?

Next time you hold a book in your hands, stop and think. Like most other things in the modern world, it is the result of thousands of years of human invention.

First, came the invention of writing, probably about 5,500 years ago. With writing, people did not have to remember everything in their heads. They could communicate with people that they never saw and share their knowledge with future generations.

Later, the Greeks were known throughout the ancient world for their literature, philosophy and science, but their 'books' looked very different from the books of today. They were called scrolls. They were difficult to use and took a lot of space in a library. It was only about 2,000 years ago that books with lots of pages were invented. With the help of an index at the back, readers could find information more quickly than in a scroll. Before long, scrolls were a thing of the past.

For more than a thousand years, the pages of books were made from animal skin. That changed in the thirteenth century, when Europeans learned about a useful Chinese invention: paper.

But the biggest change for books came in 1439, when Johannes Gutenberg invented the printing press. Before that, books were copied by hand, so they were very expensive. Many more people could afford the books that were produced on a printing press.

These days it is difficult to imagine a world without books. But human invention does not stop. Every year, more stories are bought as e-books and read on a screen.

Will anyone turn the pages of a traditional book in the future, or will books, like scrolls, soon disappear?

2 Read the magazine article quickly to check.

3 🔊 3.35 Read the article again. Are these sentences true (T) or false (F)?

1 The ancient Greeks were famous because they invented writing. *F*
2 Greek books had lots of pages.
3 There were libraries in the ancient world.
4 The first books with pages were made of animal skin.
5 Paper was invented in Europe.
6 Johannes Gutenberg's printing press produced very expensive books.

4 🔊 3.35 Read the article again. Answer the questions.

1 What did people have to do before the invention of writing?
   They had to remember everything in their heads.
2 What two problems were there with scrolls?
3 What could readers of books do better than readers of scrolls?
4 What did people use to make books when they stopped using animal skin?
5 Why was the printing press an important invention?
6 Why might books disappear in the future?

Listening

1 What are the advantages and disadvantages of reading on a smartphone?

2 🔊 3.36 Listen to the conversation. Do they talk about any of your ideas in Exercise 1?

🔊 Listening Bank Unit 9 page 120

3 In pairs, ask and answer.

1 Do you like these types of story?
   - fantasy
   - funny
   - historical
   - horror
   - romantic
   - science fiction
2 How many books do you read every year?
3 Do you prefer reading a traditional book or an e-book? Why?
4 Do you think there will be any traditional books fifty years from now? Why?/Why not?

I like fantasy and romantic stories, but I don't like horror or science fiction stories.

Writing   An opinion essay

1 Read the Writing File.

Writing File   How to write an opinion essay

In an opinion essay, you need:

- **a title**
- **an introduction giving your opinion** *(In my opinion, …)*
- **reasons for your opinion, given in a good order** *(First, … , Second, … , Finally, …)* **with examples** *(for example, …)*
- **a conclusion** *(In conclusion, …)*

2 Read Alisha's essay. Find words and expressions from the Writing File.

The most useful invention for teenagers
by Alisha Kent

In my opinion, the most useful invention for teenagers is the smartphone.

First, it's great in an emergency. If someone has an accident or there's a fire, you can phone quickly for help. Because of this, parents often feel more relaxed if you have a smartphone with you and you can stay out longer with your friends.

Second, you can use it to go online when you aren't at home. This is useful in many situations. For example, you can find out the time of the next bus when you're in a café and look at a map on the internet when you're lost.

Finally, a smartphone is great entertainment. You can watch films on it, play games, listen to music and read stories. With a smartphone in your pocket, you never have to be bored, even on a long journey.

In conclusion, the smartphone is a fantastic invention. Teenagers are happier and more independent because of it.

3 Put these parts of an opinion essay in the correct order.

a In conclusion, Edison's inventions were some of the most useful in the world.
b Second, he invented a way to bring electricity to people's homes.
c In my opinion, the world's greatest inventor was Thomas Edison.
d The world's greatest inventor *1*
e First, he invented the light bulb.
f Finally, he invented a machine that could record and play sound.

4 Read Alisha's essay again. Answer the questions.

1 In Alisha's opinion, what is the most useful invention?
The smartphone.
2 What is her main reason for choosing this invention?
3 In what two situations is this invention particularly useful?
4 How are teenagers' lives different because of it?

5 You are going to write an essay with this title:

The most important invention of the last 200 years

Choose an invention and make notes about why it is important. Use the questions in Exercise 4 to help you.

- car • computer • internet • plane • TV

6 Now write your essay. Use 'My essay' and your notes from Exercise 5.

My essay

Paragraph 1
Introduce the invention.

Paragraphs 2–4
Give reasons why the invention is important – one reason for each paragraph. Include examples of situations that prove your point.

Paragraph 5
Summarise your reasons for choosing this invention.

Remember!
- Give an introduction with your opinion.
- Give reasons for your opinion.
- Write a conclusion.
- Use words you've practised in this unit.
- Check your grammar, spelling and punctuation.

Refresh Your Memory!

Grammar Review

1 Complete the sentences with the correct passive form (Present simple or Past simple) of the verbs.

1 She *was interviewed* (interview) on the news yesterday.
2 Excuse me! .... (dogs/allow) on the bus?
3 I can't read that. It .... (write) in French.
4 .... (the internet/use) in the 1950s?
5 That word .... (not spell) correctly. Use a dictionary!
6 Too many trees .... (cut down) every year.
7 The washing-up .... (not do) last night.
8 Skateboards .... (invent) in the USA in the 1950s.

2 Make sentences and questions in the passive. Only use *by* + noun if necessary.

1 They play football in the park every Saturday.
Football is played in the park every Saturday.

2 Do people read books at your school?
3 James broke my pen.
4 They don't speak Japanese in Thailand.
5 My granny made this jumper.
6 We didn't need the tent.
7 Did they make these computers in China?
8 Our friend designed the website.

3 Active or passive? Complete the text with the correct form of the verbs.

In 1901, American inventors Wilbur and Orville Wright [1] *built* (build) a flying machine, but it [2] .... (not design) well enough. It [3] .... (not fly)! 'Man will fly, but not in our lifetime,' Wilbur [4] .... (say) sadly. The brothers [5] .... (learn) from their mistakes, however. In 1903 some changes [6] .... (made) to the design and a new machine [7] .... (build). Wilbur [8] .... (carry) through the air for 59 seconds in the new machine. Some photos [9] .... (take) of this famous moment – the flight of the world's first plane! Today, the names of the Wright brothers [10] .... (know) all around the world and thousands of people [11] .... (come) to see their plane at the museum in Washington where it [12] .... (keep).

Vocabulary Review

4 Match the beginnings (1–8) to the endings (a–h) of the sentences.

1 You can't write on your computer without a
2 We can communicate by
3 The torch won't work without a
4 A bicycle has got two
5 Please don't press those
6 You can switch on the TV with a
7 Posters are often sold in a
8 Plug the cable into the

a tube.
b mobile phone.
c remote control.
d wheels.
e keyboard.
f socket.
g battery.
h buttons.

5 Complete the sentences with the correct form of the words.

1 Claude Monet was a famous French *painter* (paint).
2 What .... (produce) is Apple™ famous for?
3 Her .... (write) is very difficult to read.
4 I love his .... (design) for the new school building.
5 The .... (build) has to make a new roof for the house.
6 Everyone thinks it's a useful .... (invent).

Speaking Review

6))) 3.37 Complete the conversation with the correct form of these words. Then listen and check.

| check | go | not work |
| problem | try | wrong |

Dad It's time to practise your electric guitar!
Boy I can't. It [1] *isn't working*.
Dad What's the [2] .... ?
Boy It can only play really quietly. Listen!
Dad There might be something [3] .... with the cable. Have you [4] .... it?
Boy But it's new. It was only bought yesterday.
Dad Er … Have you [5] .... plugging it in?
Boy Oh, silly me! Here [6] .... . Yay! It's working!

Dictation

7))) 3.38 Listen and write in your notebook.

✓ **My assessment profile:** Workbook page 135

Science File

Did you know that 0.039% of the gas in the Earth's atmosphere is carbon dioxide (CO_2)? CO_2 is a greenhouse gas: it absorbs infrared radiation. Because of this, too much CO_2 in the atmosphere causes global warming.

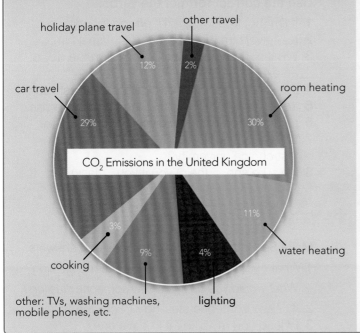

CO_2 Emissions in the United Kingdom

- holiday plane travel 12%
- other travel 2%
- car travel 29%
- room heating 30%
- water heating 11%
- lighting 4%
- other: TVs, washing machines, mobile phones, etc. 9%
- cooking 3%

CO_2 is produced when fossil fuels are burned. The average person in the United Kingdom causes 13,000 kg of carbon dioxide emissions every year (see chart). The world average is 5,800 kg. If our emissions continue, many islands and lowland areas might disappear under the sea, many parts of the world might become desert and the plants and animals that live in the oceans and on ice might die.

CO_2 is absorbed by trees and changed into oxygen. However, the average tree absorbs only 10 kg of CO_2 in a year. We would need 1,300 trees per person to absorb all our CO_2 emissions, but there are only 59 trees per person in the world. Every year 25 million trees are cut down and only 3.4 million trees are planted.

The average modern car produces 15% less CO_2 than a car that was built 10 years ago. Many new water heaters, computers and other machines also produce less CO_2 than older designs. But we use more hot water, drive further and switch on our machines for longer each year, so we are producing more CO_2, not less.

Key Words

atmosphere	greenhouse gas
absorb	infrared radiation
fossil fuel	emission
heater	

Reading

1))) 3.39 **Read the text and look at the chart. Are the sentences true (T) or false (F)?**

1 British people cause more CO_2 emissions than the world average. *T*
2 Plane travel causes more CO_2 emissions than car travel.
3 Trees change CO_2 into oxygen.
4 There are more people in the world than trees.
5 New designs of car produce more CO_2 than old designs.
6 We produce less CO_2 than we did in the past.

2))) 3.40 **Liam is giving a presentation to his class. Listen and match his notes (1–4) to (a–d).**

What could I do to produce less CO_2 when I travel?

1 My car's emissions:
2 If I rode my bike to football:
3 If we took three friends to school in our car:
4 If I got up early on Mondays:

a 1.6 kg less CO_2 per week
b 15 kg less CO_2 per week
c 600 g less CO_2 per week
d 200 g of CO_2 per km

My Science File

3 **Find out what you can do to produce less CO_2 in one of these areas.**

- around the house
- communication
- entertainment
- food
- travel

4 **Prepare a presentation for the class, giving your ideas for producing less CO_2. Then give your presentation.**

3 Review

Grammar *be going to*

1 Make questions and answers.

1 What / you / do / next weekend?

What are you going to do next weekend?

2 I / play tennis.
3 Karin / tidy the house.
4 Jo and Rory / do judo.
5 They / not / do any housework.
6 Martha / not / study.
7 What / Mum / make for dinner?
8 She / not / cook.
9 We / go out / for dinner!
10 you / have a pizza?

will or *be going to*

2 Complete the sentences with *will* or *be going to*.

1 I've decided what to give Mum for her birthday. I*'m going to* buy her some flowers.
2 It .... rain, I think. Look at those clouds.
3 A Do you think you .... be famous one day?
4 B Yes, because I .... be a very successful pop singer!
5 A Where .... you go in the summer holidays?
6 B I .... go to Thailand.
7 A How .... I know when you get there?
8 B I .... send you a text message!
9 A The menu looks good. Have you decided what you .... have?
10 B Hmm. I think I .... have the chicken pie.

First conditional

3 Complete the First conditional sentences. Use the correct form of the verbs.

1 If I*'m* (be) free tonight, I*'ll phone* (phone) you.
2 I .... (give) him the message if I .... (see) him.
3 What .... (happen) if you .... (be) ill on the day of an exam?
4 If it .... (rain), we .... (not sit) outside at the restaurant.
5 You .... (not get) fit if you .... (not do) any exercise.
6 I .... (text) you if you .... (give) me your number.
7 Where .... (you go) if you .... (not get) into your first choice university?
8 I'm sure she .... (help) you if you .... (ask) her.

Second conditional

4 Make Second conditional questions and answers.

1 What / you do / if you / see / someone stealing?

What would you do if you saw someone stealing?

2 If I / see someone stealing / I / call the police.
3 I / lend you my bike / if I / have one.
4 If Carrie / work harder / she / pass her exams.
5 If you / come home late, your parents / be angry?
6 I / walk away / if someone / be / rude to me.
7 If it / not raining / I / go for a walk.
8 What / you do / if you / forget / your mum's birthday?
9 If I / forget my mum's birthday / I / be very sad.

Relative pronouns

5 Complete the sentences. Use *where*, *which* or *who*.

1 These are the shoes *which* were very expensive.
2 The woman .... is in hospital is our teacher.
3 The sandwich .... I made was delicious.
4 Picasso is the artist .... painted that picture.
5 That's the café .... we go at weekends.
6 The suitcase .... is very heavy is mine!
7 The dog .... barks all the time is very annoying.
8 Liverpool is the city .... we saw a big football match.

Present simple passive

6 **Complete the sentences with the Present simple passive form of the verbs.**

1 Every day, millions of text messages *are sent*. (send)
2 The winners .... after the contest. (announce)
3 The windows .... every two months. (clean)
4 In our school, students who misbehave .... detention. (give)
5 Ice cream .... from milk. (make)
6 Every season a new football team captain .... . (choose)
7 A lot of the world's olive oil .... in Spain. (produce)
8 How often .... complaints about customer service .... ? (receive)

Past simple passive

7 **Make sentences in the Past simple passive.**

1 When / pizzas / first / invent?
When were pizzas first invented?
2 Where / the first Olympic Games / hold?
3 What / yo-yos / first / use for?
4 Why / the Globe Theatre / rebuild?
5 The airport / close / because of bad weather.
6 The criminal / send / to prison.
7 I / give / some money for my birthday.
8 you / invite / to their wedding?

Speaking Persuading

1 **Complete the conversation with these words.**

be fun	better than	come on
don't know	I'll do	sure you

A I don't feel like going to the Tango dancing class tonight.
B Oh, ¹*come on*, Alice! It'll ² .... !
A I ³ .... . I'm terrible at dancing.
B I'm ⁴ .... aren't. Anyway, we're all beginners. Please come. It'll be ⁵ .... staying at home all alone.
A OK. ⁶ .... it. Just don't laugh at me when I fall over!

Talking about health

2 **Put the conversation in the correct order.**

.... No, I'm fine. I'll just rest here for a bit.
.1. Ow!
.... I can see that by the way you're walking … Here, sit down for a bit. How does that feel?
.... What's the matter, Rosie?
.... A bit better, thanks.
.... Perhaps you've sprained it. Shall I call the doctor?
.... I've got a pain in my knee all of a sudden.

Problems with machines

3 **Make the conversation.**

1 **A** I / borrow your digital camera?
Can I borrow your digital camera?
2 **B** Sorry, / it / not / work.
3 **A** What / problem / with it?
4 **B** There / might / something / wrong / battery.
5 **A** you / check / it?
6 **B** Yes, I / have.
7 **A** You / try / take / it out? And putting it back in again?
8 **B** No, I / haven't. I / try / that now.

Vocabulary Protest and support

1 Choose the correct option.

1 Please sign our *banner / petition*. We are collecting signatures of people who are against the proposed new motorway.
2 The roads are closed because of a large student *demonstration / donation*.
3 We are making *placards / charities* to hold up when we go on the *sit-in / march* through the streets.
4 The *slogan / collection* of our protest movement is, 'Do you call this progress?'
5 We're organising a *sit-in / fundraising event* for a *banner / charity* called Children in Need.
6 We need people to distribute leaflets about our organisation. Would you like to be a *placard / volunteer*?
7 Please make a generous *slogan / donation* to our *collection / petition* for blind people.

Verb + preposition

2 Complete the sentences with the correct prepositions.

1 I'm sorry, I don't agree *with* you.
2 Do you care .... the environment?
3 The government insists .... going ahead with plans for a new airport.
4 I must apologise .... my late arrival.
5 Do you ever worry .... the future?
6 What are the students protesting .... ?
7 We all hope .... a solution to the problem of global warming.
8 Do you ever argue .... your parents about homework?

Extreme adjectives

3 Complete the sentences with extreme adjectives.

1 It wasn't just small – it was *tiny*.
2 It was really cold – .... , in fact.
3 We weren't just tired after the hike. We were .... .
4 Was the film good? Yes! It was really .... .
5 It wasn't just scary – it was .... .
6 Bad? It was much worse than that. It was absolutely .... .

Illness and injury

4 Choose the correct option.

1 I ate too much and now I've got a *sprained ankle / stomachache*.
2 I need to go the dentist. I've got *toothache / a headache*.
3 Look at these spots all over my arms. It's some kind of *cough / rash*.
4 Your *burn / temperature* is very high – look, it shows 39°C on the thermometer.
5 I've got such a *backache / sore throat* – it really hurts when I eat.
6 I've got a bad *cold / cut* on my finger. It's bleeding a lot.

Machine nouns and verbs

5 Choose the correct option.

1 *Plug / Attach* the machine into the socket.
2 *Attach / Press* the cable into the back of the machine.
3 *Produce / Press* the button to start the machine.
4 Do you know how energy is *communicated / produced*?
5 We usually *invent / communicate* by email or text.
6 You should always *plug in / switch off* machines when they aren't in use.

Word building

6 Complete the text with the correct form of the words.

The ¹ *inventors* (invent) of the first hot air balloon were the Montgolfier brothers. They ² .... (build) the balloon in 1793. The idea for the ³ .... (invent) came when they burned some paper. The fire ⁴ .... (product) hot air which made the paper float up into the air. Later, they ⁵ .... (designer) a balloon from cloth and paper. They made a fire under it. The first passengers were a duck, a sheep and a chicken.

Word list

Unit 7   Make A Difference

Protest and support

banner	/ˈbænə/
charity	/ˈtʃærəti/
collection	/kəˈlekʃən/
demonstration	/ˌdemənˈstreɪʃən/
donation	/dəʊˈneɪʃən/
fundraising event	/ˈfʌndreɪzɪŋ ɪˌvent/
march (n)	/mɑːtʃ/
petition (n)	/pəˈtɪʃən/
placard	/ˈplækɑːd/
sit-in (n)	/ˈsɪt ɪn/
slogan	/ˈsləʊgən/
volunteer (n)	/ˌvɒlənˈtɪə/

Verb + preposition

agree with	/əˈgriː wɪð, wɪθ/
apologise for	/əˈpɒlədʒaɪz fə, fɔː/
argue with	/ˈɑːgjuː wɪð, wɪθ/
believe in	/bɪˈliːv ɪn/
care about	/ˈkeər əˌbaʊt/
decide on	/dɪˈsaɪd ɒn/
disapprove of	/ˌdɪsəˈpruːv əv/
hope for	/ˈhəʊp fə, fɔː/
insist on	/ɪnˈsɪst ɒn/
know about	/ˈnəʊ əˌbaʊt/
protest about	/prəˈtest əˌbaʊt/
worry about	/ˈwʌri əˌbaʊt/

Unit 8   Danger And Risk

Extreme adjectives

awful	/ˈɔːfəl/
boiling	/ˈbɔɪlɪŋ/
brilliant	/ˈbrɪljənt/
exhausted	/ɪgˈzɔːstəd/
freezing	/ˈfriːzɪŋ/
furious	/ˈfjʊəriəs/
huge	/hjuːdʒ/
terrifying	/ˈterəfaɪ-ɪŋ/
thrilled	/θrɪld/
tiny	/ˈtaɪni/

Illness and injury

a burn	/bɜːn/
a cold	/kəʊld/
a cough	/kɒf/
a cut	/kʌt/
a headache	/ˈhedeɪk/
a rash	/ræʃ/
a sore throat	/ˌsɔː ˈθrəʊt/
a sprained ankle	/ˌspreɪnd ˈæŋkəl/
a stomachache	/ˈstʌmək-eɪk/
a temperature	/ˈtemprətʃə/
backache	/ˈbækeɪk/
toothache	/ˈtuːθeɪk/

Unit 9   Inventions

Machine nouns and verbs

Verbs

attach	/əˈtætʃ/
build	/bɪld/
communicate	/kəˈmjuːnɪkeɪt/
invent	/ɪnˈvent/
press	/pres/
plug in	/ˌplʌg ˈɪn/
produce	/prəˈdjuːs/
switch off	/ˌswɪtʃ ˈɒf/
switch on	/ˌswɪtʃ ˈɒn/

Nouns

battery	/ˈbætəri/
button	/ˈbʌtn/
cable	/ˈkeɪbəl/
keyboard	/ˈkiːbɔːd/
remote control	/rɪˌməʊt kənˈtrəʊl/
socket	/ˈsɒkət/
tube	/tjuːb/
wheel	/wiːl/

Word building

build	/bɪld/
builder	/ˈbɪldə/
building	/ˈbɪldɪŋ/
design	/dɪˈzaɪn/
designer	/dɪˈzaɪnə/
design	/dɪˈzaɪn/
invent	/ɪnˈvent/
inventor	/ɪnˈventə/
invention	/ɪnˈvenʃən/
paint	/peɪnt/
painter	/ˈpeɪntə/
painting	/ˈpeɪntɪŋ/
produce	/prəˈdjuːs/
producer	/prəˈdjuːsə/
product	/ˈprɒdʌkt/
write	/raɪt/
writer	/ˈraɪtə/
writing	/ˈraɪtɪŋ/

Brain Trainers

Unit 1

Spot the difference

1   Look at the photo on page 14 for one minute. Now study this photo. What differences can you spot?

Vocabulary

2a Find the odd word out in each box. You have one minute.

> wall   roof   ceiling
> garage   **f**loor

> **a**ttic   stairs
> hall   cella**r**   offic**e**

> landi**n**g   lawn   bal**c**ony
> **p**atio   driv**e**

2b Arrange the letters in bold to make a new home word.

3   Look at the objects in the grid for one minute. Cover the grid and write the words in your notebook. How many can you remember?

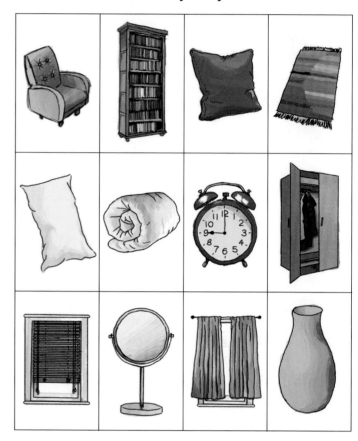

Unit 2

Spot the difference

1   Look at the photo on page 24 for one minute. Now study this photo. What differences can you spot?

Vocabulary

2   Make words. Each word has three shapes.

inte-rest-ing

3   Work in pairs. Say an adjective. Your partner says the adjective and correct preposition. Then change roles.

| proud | angry | keen | | bad | tired | excited |
| bored | sorry | interested | good | afraid | popular |

Unit 3

Spot the difference

1   Look at the photo on page 34 for one minute. Now study this photo. What differences can you spot?

Vocabulary

2   Work in pairs. Student A chooses a shopping word. Student B asks Student A the questions below. Student B guesses the word.

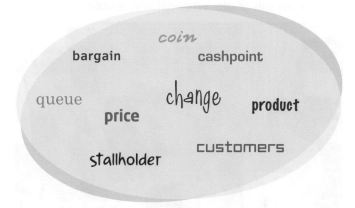

Questions
How many syllables are there?
How many letters are there?
How many vowels are there?

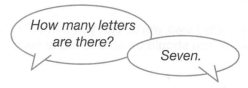

3a   Complete the five pairs of money verbs below. You've got one minute.

b_y   s_ _l
s_ v_   sp_ _d
w_n   e_ _n
c_ s_   _ff_ _d
l_ _d   b_ _r_ w

3b   Complete the sentence with two more money verbs.

You can pay for things in c_ _h or by c_ _ _ _t c _ _ _ .

Brain Trainers

Unit 4

Spot the difference

1 Look at the photo on page 48 for one minute. Now study this photo. What differences can you spot?

Vocabulary

2 How many *news* words can you think of in one minute? You should be able to make seven.

1 *local news*

3a Read the pairs of words aloud three times. Cover them and read the list below. Which word is missing?

> quietly → **loudly**   **carefully** → carelessly
>
> **happily** → sadly   **patiently** → angrily

carefully	angrily	loudly	happily
quietly	patiently	carelessly	

3b Now make more adverbs using the different coloured letters. Then match the opposites.

well - badly

Unit 5

Spot the difference

1 Look at the photo on page 58 for one minute. Now study this photo. What differences can you spot?

Vocabulary

2 Look at the pictures for two minutes. Try to remember them in order. Then cover them. Take turns to make suggestions. Can you remember all nine?

3a Find six meanings for the verb *get* in the puzzle. You have two minutes.

3b Think of one more meaning for the verb *get*.

b	g	h	s	p	n	r
f	e	t	c	h	r	e
b	a	c	m	i	d	c
p	u	l	o	c	r	e
w	h	y	v	m	k	i
f	u	r	e	n	e	v
e	a	r	r	i	v	e

Unit 6
Spot the difference

1 Look at the photo on page 68 for one minute. Now study this photo. What differences can you spot?

Vocabulary

2 Work in small groups. Choose an activity from the box. Act it out. Your classmates guess the activity.

do the washing-up	feed the cat
lay the table	hang out the washing
do the ironing	make the bed
cook a meal	run the washing machine
wash the car	sweep the floor

3 Look at the faces carefully. Match them with the feeling adjectives. Write the answers in your notebooks. Then check your answers on page 117.

relaxed	confused	nervous	upset
confident	disappointed	embarrassed	fed up

1 *fed up*

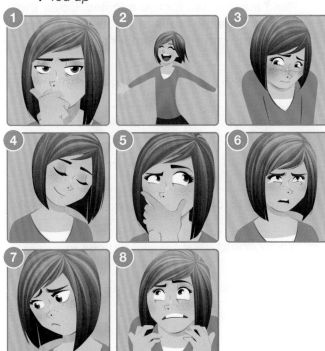

Brain Trainers

Unit 7

Spot the difference

1   Look at the photo on page 82 for one minute. Now study this photo. What differences can you spot?

Vocabulary

2   How many protest words and phrases can you think of with the letter *n* in them? Think of nine.

a banner

3   Read the phrases for two minutes. Cover the list and write the phrases in your notebook. How many can you remember?

care about	argue with
hope for	apologise for
decide on	worry about
disapprove of	agree with
know about	believe in
protest against	insist on

Unit 8

Spot the difference

1   Look at the photo on page 92 for one minute. Now study this photo. What differences can you spot?

Vocabulary

2   Look at the photos. Use an extreme adjective to describe each one. You have two minutes.

1 *huge*

Which two extreme adjectives are missing?

3 Work in small groups. Choose an illness or injury. Act it out. Your classmates guess the problem.

Have you got a cut on your hand?

No.

Have you got a burn?

Yes, I have!

Unit 9

Spot the difference

1 Look at the photo on page 102 for one minute. Now study this photo. What differences can you spot?

Vocabulary

2a Read the coloured words aloud three times. Cover them and read the list below. Which word is missing?

cable	button	communicate
plug in	press	switch on	keyboard

plug in	socket	press	button
switch on	keyboard	cable	communicate

2b Now try again.

attach	remote control	tube
battery	wheel	invent	build

invent	wheel	build	battery
attach	tube	switch off	remote control

3a Make words. Each word has three shapes.
in-ven-tor

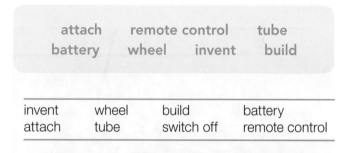

3b Now say what each person does. What is the result of their work?

An inventor ....

The result is ....

Listening Bank 🔊

Unit 1

1 🔊 1.11 **Listen again. Listen to the description of Hannah's room and what that says about her personality.**

pale walls – talkative

2 🔊 1.11 **Listen again. Complete the sentences.**
1 Hannah's walls are pale *yellow*.
2 There's a bright green .... on the bed.
3 She .... trying new experiences.
4 She's got pictures of .... and friends on the walls.
5 Her room is quite .... at the moment.
6 Her .... likes cleaning up in her room.

Unit 2

1 🔊 1.24 **Listen again. Choose the correct option.**
1 The picture is *real / fake*.
2 The men were *800 / 11,000* feet above the streets.
3 The men were working in *Slovakia / America*.
4 Gusti Popovic is the man *on the right / on the left*.
5 He sent *a letter / a postcard* with the photo.
6 Gusti Popovic was *good at / bad at* his job.

2 🔊 1.24 **Listen again. Answer the questions.**
1 Does the boy think the photo is real at first?
No, he doesn't.

2 What does the girl say about Charles Ebbets?
3 What does the boy ask about the men?
4 How does the girl identify Gusti Popovic?
5 Does she say he sent his wife a photo?

Unit 3

1 🔊 1.36 **Listen again. What do these numbers refer to?**
1 16 *the age of the boy*
2 £95
3 2
4 20
5 65,000

2 🔊 1.36 **Listen again and complete the sentences.**
1 The boy bought a *console* and two games online.
2 The console arrived in the .... .
3 There were lots of 20 euro .... in the box.
4 The boy and his parents talked to the .... .
5 They were worried the money came from .... .
6 The police want to find the owner of the .... .

Unit 4

1 🔊 2.11 **Listen. Match the speakers (1–3) to the opinions (a–c).**
Speaker 1
Speaker 2
Speaker 3

a I'm not interested in international news. It's not important to me.
b The news is usually bad. It's often about wars or natural disasters.
c It's good to know what is happening in the world.

2 🔊 2.11 **Listen again. Choose the correct options.**
1 Speaker 1 *has read / hasn't read* the news today.
2 He *sometimes / often* reads his dad's newspaper.
3 He *has / hasn't* got time to read the paper every day.
4 Speaker 2 listened to the news *on the radio / on TV*.
5 She thinks there was a headline about *politicians / world leaders* meeting.
6 She *can / can't* remember all of today's headlines.
7 Speaker 3 read the headlines *in a newspaper / on a news website*.
8 Manchester United are playing Chelsea next *month / week*.
9 Speaker 3 is interested in *sports reports / general news*.

Unit 5

1 🔊 **2.22** **Listen. Choose the correct answers.**

1 Which country has Troy just visited?
  a *Fiji*
  b Japan
  c Turkey

2 What can you do in the first hotel?
  a open the windows
  b feed the fish
  c go swimming

3 What can you find in the second hotel?
  a an alarm clock
  b big windows
  c a large bed

4 What are rooms at the third hotel like?
  a dark and wet
  b warm and comfortable
  c very small

5 Which place does Troy recommend for a holiday?
  a Fiji
  b Japan
  c Turkey

2 🔊 **2.22** **Listen again. Answer the questions.**

1 Where was the hotel in Fiji?
  25 metres under the sea
2 What has each room in the hotel got?
3 What's unusual about the hotel in Japan?
4 Are there any beds in the hotel?
5 Where is the hotel in Cappadocia?
6 Why does Troy recommend Cappadocia for a holiday?

Unit 6

1 🔊 **2.35** **Listen again. Choose the correct options.**

Conversation 1
1 The boy thinks the girl should wear
  a trousers.   **b** shorts.   **c** *a dress*.
2 The girl can't wear this because it's
  a not small enough.   **b** too small.   **c** horrible.

Conversation 2
3 The boy has to
  a clear the table.
  b hang out the washing
  c lay the table.
4 The boy is feeling
  a grateful.   **b** glad.   **c** fed up.

Conversation 3
5 The boy wants to go to a party with
  a his dad.   **b** football players.   **c** his mum.
6 He can't go to the party because it's too
  a late.   **b** expensive.   **c** far away.

Conversation 4
7 The girl is having problems with
  a her English.   **b** her computer.   **c** her Maths.
8 The boy thinks she should
  a learn from him.
  b learn from his teacher.
  c become a teacher.

Cappadocia

Listening Bank

Unit 7

1 🔊 **3.9** Listen again. Complete the information leaflet.

Family **Shoebox Appeal**

How to prepare a box

1. Choose a ¹ *shoebox*.
2. Fill ² .... with gifts.
3. Put ³ .... in the box. This pays for transport.
4. Take your box to the Shoebox collection point.

What's in a box?

- things for ⁴ ...., e.g. notebooks, pencils
- other useful things: a toothbrush, ⁵ ....

Don't put in:

- medicine, ⁶ .... or scissors.

Unit 8

1 🔊 **3.23** Listen again. Choose the correct options to complete the advert.

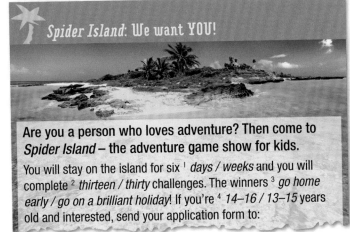

Spider Island: We want YOU!

Are you a person who loves adventure? Then come to *Spider Island* **– the adventure game show for kids.**

You will stay on the island for six ¹ *days / weeks* and you will complete ² *thirteen / thirty* challenges. The winners ³ *go home early / go on a brilliant holiday*! If you're ⁴ *14–16 / 13–15* years old and interested, send your application form to:

2 🔊 **3.23** Listen again. Are these sentences true (T) or false (F)?

1. The girl saw an announcement in a magazine. *F*
2. The girl and boy both watch the show.
3. The show is on a desert island.
4. The boy is worried about the challenges.
5. The girl is interested in the prize.
6. They can both apply for the show.

Unit 9

1 🔊 **3.36** Listen to the conversation. What advantages and disadvantages of reading on a smartphone did the speakers mention?

2 🔊 **3.36** Listen again. Are these sentences true (T) or false (F)?

1. The boy read a horror story on his smartphone. *F*
2. The boy reads at the bus stop.
3. He likes carrying books with him because they're small.
4. The girl thinks smartphone screens are a good size for reading.
5. The boy has got thirteen e-books on his smartphone.
6. The girl likes keeping her books for years.

3 Correct the false sentences from Exercise 2.

1. *The boy read a science fiction story on his smartphone.*

Reading

1 🔊 3.41 Read about Homes in the UK. Are there a lot of very tall buildings in British cities?

2 Read about Homes in the UK again. Are the sentences true (T) or false (F)? Correct the false sentences.

1 Terraced houses usually have a big garden.
2 Thirty-two percent of homes in the UK are semi-detached houses.
3 Cellars are more usual than attics in detached houses.
4 There are a lot of flats in cities.

3 In pairs, answer the questions.

1 In your area, what type of home do most people live in?
2 Which of these things are usual in homes in your area?
   • an attic • a balcony • a cellar
   • a garage • a garden
3 Think of another part of your country. What type of homes are popular there?
4 Are there many very tall buildings in big cities? Are they homes, offices or both?

4 Write a short paragraph about homes in your country. Use your answers to Exercise 3 and the Homes in the UK examples to help you.

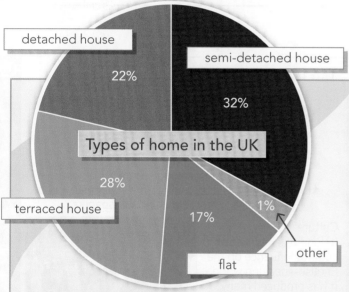

detached house — 22%

semi-detached house — 32%

Types of home in the UK

terraced house — 28%

flat — 17%

other — 1%

Terraced houses
A lot of families live in terraced houses. They share the walls with the houses next to them. The living room is often at the front of the house, next to the hall and the kitchen is at the back. The bedrooms and bathroom are upstairs.
Terraced houses don't often have a garage, but there's usually a small garden at the back. If you want a good game of football, however, go to the park!

Semi-detached houses
There are more 'semis' in the UK than any other type of house. They are two houses next to each other. They share a wall on one side and you can walk round to the garden on the other side. It's very important to be friends with your next-door neighbours!

Detached houses
Detached houses are popular with families, but there aren't many in cities. They usually have three or four bedrooms upstairs and they often have a big garden and a garage. A lot of them have attics, but only a small number of older houses have cellars.

Flats
A lot of people in cities live in flats. Some are in big buildings, but others are on one floor of a terraced house. They sometimes have small balconies.
Very tall buildings are unusual in British cities. The highest flat in the UK is in the Beetham Tower in Manchester. It is on the 47th floor.

The Beetham Tower

Reading

1 ◎ 3.42 **Read about the Republic of Ireland. Which of these things are mentioned?**

business	dancing	mountains	religion
technology	tradition	TV	

2 **Read about the Republic of Ireland again and choose the correct options.**

1 *All / Some* of Ireland is in the United Kingdom.
2 Irish is the main language in *some / all* schools in Ireland.
3 In Irish dancing, you have to move your *feet / arms* very fast.
4 Some people say that *not many / many* Irish people talk a lot.

3 **In pairs, answer the questions.**

1 Was your country ever ruled by another country? Which one? Did this change your language or other parts of your culture?
2 What type of dancing is your country famous for? Have you ever tried it?
3 Is there anywhere in your country that has a strange tradition? What is it?

4 **Write a short paragraph about your country. Use your answers to Exercise 3 and the Republic of Ireland examples to help you.**

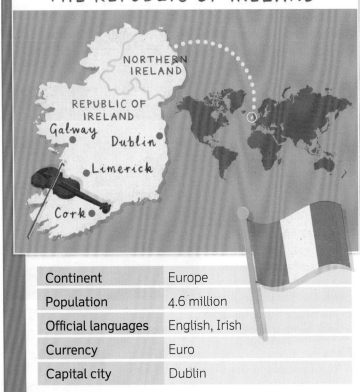

THE REPUBLIC OF IRELAND

NORTHERN IRELAND

REPUBLIC OF IRELAND

Galway

Dublin

Limerick

Cork

Continent	Europe
Population	4.6 million
Official languages	English, Irish
Currency	Euro
Capital city	Dublin

North and South

For many centuries Ireland was ruled by the English, but in the early twentieth century, most of the island became an independent country, the Republic of Ireland. Northern Ireland, however, continued to be part of the United Kingdom. The two parts of Ireland have a shared culture, but there are some religious differences. In the north, most people are Protestants; in the south, most people are Catholics.

This is a shamrock – the symbol of Ireland

Language

Only about one percent of the population now speaks Irish as their main language at home. Most people speak English. However, more and more children are going to Irish-speaking schools and there are several Irish TV channels, radio stations and newspapers.

Culture

Ireland has had a strong cultural influence on the English-speaking world. It has produced many great writers, including Oscar Wilde and George Bernard Shaw; actors, including Pierce Brosnan and Colin Farrell; and musicians, including U2. Irish step dancing – fast foot movements while the body and arms don't move – has also become popular around the world.

The Gift of the Gab

At Blarney Castle in the south of Ireland, you can find the Blarney Stone. According to tradition, if you kiss this special stone you will have the 'gift of the gab' – the ability to talk well and persuade people easily. Some people think that the Irish are the most talkative people in the world. Have they all kissed the Blarney Stone?

Reading

1 🔊 3.43 **Read about Sports in the UK. Which sport:**

1 is the UK's favourite?
2 is popular in summer?
3 is popular with older people?
4 shares its name with a school?

2 **Read about Sports in the UK again. Answer the questions.**

1 How long are the longest cricket matches?
2 In football, what important things happened in the UK before they happened in other countries?
3 What three differences are there between football and rugby?
4 Why did the king make playing golf illegal?

Your culture

3 **In pairs, answer the questions.**

1 Are any of the sports on this page popular in your country? Which ones? Are you a fan of these sports?
2 What sports started in your country? Do you like playing or watching them?
3 What are the most important sporting events in your country? Where and when do they happen?

4 **Write a short paragraph about sports in your country. Use your answers to Exercise 3 and the Sports in the UK examples to help you.**

SPORTS in the UK

Cricket

Cricket began in England about four hundred years ago and today there are cricket matches all over the country on summer weekends. A local match takes all afternoon. Professional games at famous stadiums like Lord's in London can last for five days and there is often no winner at the end. People play cricket in most English-speaking countries and it is very popular in India and Pakistan.

Football

The UK was the first country in the world with international football teams, professional players and a national football competition. Today football is the UK's most popular sport and the English Premier League has some of the world's most famous clubs and players. The most important match of the year is the FA Cup Final at London's Wembley Stadium.

Rugby

This sport began in a famous English school, Rugby School. It is like football, but there are some big differences. The ball is an oval shape and you can carry it as well as kick it. You can also pull players off their feet. Every year there is an important competition, the Six Nations, between the teams of England, Scotland, Wales, Ireland, France and Italy.

Golf

Golf began in Scotland. In the fifteenth century, the sport was illegal – the king was worried that it was taking too much of people's time. Later, the sport became popular around the world. Many older people play golf in the UK today and some of the best professional players are British.

Culture 4

Reading

1 🔊 **3.44** Read about Robin Hood. Are these descriptions true (T), false (F), or don't know (DK)?

a character in TV shows	a hero
a king	a real thief
the Sheriff of Nottingham	

2 Read about Robin Hood again. Answer the questions.
  1 Why did Robin Hood go to the Middle East?
  2 Why did he and his friends steal money?
  3 How long have there been stories about Robin Hood?
  4 Why do people visit the Major Oak?

Your culture

3 In pairs, answer the questions.
  1 What traditional heroes are there in your culture?
  2 What do they do in the stories about them?
  3 Are the stories true?

4 Write a short paragraph about traditional heroes in your country. Use your answers to Exercise 3 and the Robin Hood examples to help you.

Robin Hood

A statue of Robin Hood in Nottingham

The Major Oak

Robin Hood is England's most famous hero. What do we know about him?

The stories
Robin was a rich man from the north of England. He was very good at archery and went to the Middle East to fight with King Richard I. When he came home, the Sheriff of Nottingham took his lands, so he lived in Sherwood Forest with a group of friends – Little John, Will Scarlett and others. They stole money from the rich and gave it to the poor.

Are the stories true?
We don't know. There are a lot of old papers about the thieves at the end of the twelfth century, when Richard I was king. But no one has found papers about a Robin Hood in Nottingham.

Robin Hood today
Robin Hood has been the hero of songs and stories for more than six hundred years and there have been more than fifty films and TV shows about him. There is a big Robin Hood celebration in Nottingham every year.

People wear twelfth-century clothes, listen to stories and music and try archery. They also go to the Robin Hood Visitor Centre in Sherwood Forest and see a big old tree called the Major Oak. In some stories, Robin hid from the Sheriff's men inside it.

Russell Crowe as Robin Hood in the 2010 film

Culture ⑤

Reading

1 🔊 **3.45** Read about Multicultural Britain. Match the different groups of people (1–4) to these things.

curry	Diwali	Jamaica
newspapers	street festivals	the European Union

2 Read about Multicultural Britain again. Complete the sentences.

1 Four percent of the people in Britain are .... .
2 You can buy Polish .... , newspapers and .... magazines in British shops.
3 1.5 million people go to see the .... every year.
4 People with parents from different ethnic groups are called .... .

3 In pairs, answer the questions.

1 What ethnic groups are there in your country?
2 How long have they lived there?
3 Which other countries' food is popular in your country?
4 Does your country celebrate any festivals from other cultures? What are they?

4 Write a short paragraph about different cultures in your country. Use your answers to Exercise 3 and the Multicultural Britain examples to help you.

Multicultural Britain

Many new groups of people have come to Britain since the Romans arrived two thousand years ago. Some important ethnic groups in Britain are:

1 South Asian

A lot of people from India, Pakistan, Bangladesh and Sri Lanka have moved to Britain since 1950. Today, four percent of the people in Britain are South Asian and their culture has become an important part of British life. There are more Indian restaurants in Britain than fish and chip shops and curry is one of Britain's favourite meals. A lot of British schools celebrate South Asian festivals like Diwali and Eid.

2 Polish

A lot of Polish people came to Britain in the 1940s. More came after 2004, when Poland joined the European Union. About 700,000 Polish people now live in Britain. Supermarkets all over the country sell Polish food and there are several Polish-language magazines and newspapers.

3 Afro-Caribbean

Between 1948 and 1962, many thousands of people came to Britain from Jamaica, Barbados and other Caribbean islands. There are now more than 600,000 Afro-Caribbean people in Britain. The Notting Hill Carnival is a celebration of Afro-Caribbean culture in London and Europe's largest street festival. 1.5 million people go to it every August.

4 Mixed race

Ten percent of British children are mixed race – their parents come from different ethnic groups. Soon mixed race people will be the second biggest ethnic group in Britain.

◀ 125 ▶

Culture 6

Canada

Reading

1 🔊 3.46 **Read about Canada. What is the most important language in each region?**

1 Ontario
2 Quebec
3 Nunavut

2 **Read about Canada again. Complete the sentences with place names.**

1 The capital city of Canada is .... .
2 The Niagara Falls is a popular place for visitors in the .... region.
3 A lot of maple syrup comes from .... .
4 People in the town of .... don't see the sun for four months in winter.

Your culture

3 **In pairs, answer the questions.**

1 What are the most popular places in your country for visitors from other countries?
2 Are there regions in your country where the country's official language isn't the main language? Do people in these regions want to be independent? Give examples.
3 What food is your country or region famous for?
4 Are there any regions where not many people live? Why don't more people live there?

4 **Write a short paragraph about different regions in your country. Use your answers to Exercise 3 and the Canada examples to help you.**

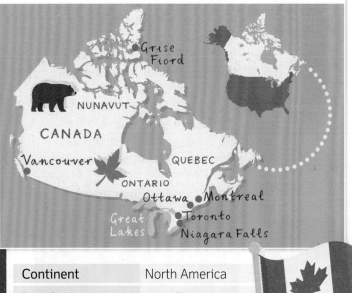

CANADA

Continent	North America
Population	35 million
Official languages	English, French
Currency	Canadian dollar
Favourite sport	Ice hockey

Canada is the world's second largest country, but a lot of the land in the centre and north is empty. Canada is famous for its cold winters and beautiful mountains.

Ontario
Canada's biggest city, Toronto, and its capital, Ottawa, are in this region. Here, as in most of Canada, English is the most important language. A lot of people come here to visit the Niagara Falls and the Great Lakes.

Quebec
Canada's second biggest city, Montreal, is here. Most people in Quebec speak French and about forty percent want Quebec to be an independent country. Most of Canada's famous 'maple syrup' comes from this region. Canadians love eating it with pancakes and even have the leaf of the maple tree on their flag.

Nunavut
Nunavut is the biggest region in Canada, but only 33,000 people live there. There are no trees and the land and sea are frozen for most of the year. It is easier to travel by snowmobile than by car. At Grise Fiord, the furthest north of Nunavut's towns, there are four months without daylight in winter and four months without night in summer. Most people in Nunavut are Inuit. They speak the Inuit language, but they don't live in igloos. They have houses with TVs and the internet.

126

Irregular verb list

Verb	Past Simple	Past Participle
be	was/were	been
become	became	become
begin	began	begun
break	broke	broken
bring	brought	brought
build	built	built
buy	bought	bought
can	could	been able
catch	caught	caught
choose	chose	chosen
come	came	come
cost	cost	cost
cut	cut	cut
do	did	done
draw	drew	drawn
drink	drank	drunk
drive	drove	driven
eat	ate	eaten
fall	fell	fallen
feed	fed	fed
feel	felt	felt
fight	fought	fought
find	found	found
fly	flew	flown
forget	forgot	forgotten
get	got	got
give	gave	given
go	went	gone/been
grow	grew	grown
have	had	had
hear	heard	heard
hold	held	held
keep	kept	kept
know	knew	known
learn	learned/learnt	learned/learnt
leave	left	left
lend	lent	lent

Verb	Past Simple	Past Participle
light	lit	lit
lose	lost	lost
make	made	made
mean	meant	meant
meet	met	met
pay	paid	paid
put	put	put
read /riːd/	read /red/	read /red/
ride	rode	ridden
ring	rang	rung
run	ran	run
say	said	said
see	saw	seen
sell	sold	sold
send	sent	sent
shine	shone	shone
show	showed	shown
sing	sang	sung
sit	sat	sat
sleep	slept	slept
speak	spoke	spoken
spell	spelled/spelt	spelled/spelt
spend	spent	spent
stand	stood	stood
steal	stole	stolen
swim	swam	swum
take	took	taken
teach	taught	taught
tell	told	told
think	thought	thought
throw	threw	thrown
understand	understood	understood
wake	woke	woken
wear	wore	worn
win	won	won
write	wrote	written

Pearson Education Limited,
Edinburgh Gate, Harlow
Essex, CM20 2JE, England
and Associated Companies throughout the world
www.pearsonelt.com

First published 2013
Fifteenth impression 2022
ISBN 978-1-4082-9363-8
Set in 10.5/12.5pt LTC Helvetica Neue Light
Printed in Slovakia by Neografia

Acknowledgements
We are grateful to the following for permission to reproduce copyright
material:
Article 1.1 adapted from www.minihousebuilder.com; Article 6.7
adapted from www.bullyingcanada.ca

In some instances we have been unable to trace the owners of
copyright material and we would appreciate any information that would
enable us to do so.

The publisher would like to thank the following for their kind permission
to reproduce their photographs:

(Key: b-bottom; c-centre; l-left; r-right; t-top)

akg-images Ltd: 104tr, Erich Lessing 104cl; **Alamy Images:** AAD
Worldwide Travel Images 20tr, Colin Palmer Photography 124tr, Ashley
Cooper 78c, CountrySideCollection - Homer Sykes 123tl, Design Pics
Inc 78bl, Gunter Marx / AE 88t, Terry Harris 31r, Bert Hoferichter 126bl,
imagebroker 20cl, Impressions / Balan Madhavan 79l, Janine Wiedel
Photolibrary 125br, David L. Moore 45, photoWORKS 121cr, Picture
Contact BV 126br, Adrian Sherratt 27b, Evan Spiler 119r, Gregory
Wrona 125bc; **Bridgeman Art Library Ltd:** Arundel Castle 104cr;
Bullying Canada: Charles Benn 73l, 73r; **Crina Coco Popescu:**
97l, 97r; **Corbis:** Alan Copson / Robert Harding World Imagery 31l,
Bettmann 118, Destinations 55tr, 122tr, Do Van Dijck / Foto Natura /
Minden Pictures 116br/7, Leonard Gertz 116br/8, Jack Hollingsworth
81, 108, Simon Jarratt 27t, Jerry Lampen / epa 94l, Ocean 20tl, 65r,
Peter Andrews / Reuters 60tr, Pool / Retna Ltd 80r, Paul Thompson
121br, David Turnley 50; **Divine Chocolate:** 87tr, Kim Naylor 87tl;
Dynamic Graphics, Inc.: 126tr; **Fotolia.com:** Aaron Amat 116br/6,
dell 72, Joe Gough 125bl, Pablo h. Caridad 19tr, Aleksandar Jocic 37,
Patryk Kosmider 120r, Miravision 62, Monia 20bl, 42, Anna Omelchenko
116br/2, Pascal Rateau 19cr, Scanrail 105, Petr Vaclavek 104tl;
Getty Images: 2009 Blixah 7, 36r, 78t, 78cl, 78br, 119l, 123tr, 123br,
Maxine Adcock 36l, AFP 60cr, 88c, Todd Bigelow 60cl, Scott Cramer
88b, DreamPictures 47, Tony Eveling 21cl, Gamma-Rapho 53tr, 53br,
Scott MacBride 20br, Regine Mahaux 12, National Geographic 99l
(Bkgd), Michael Nichols 21bl, Simon Rawles 87b, Kenneth Riley 63b,
Aurora Rodriguez 21cr, Henrik Sorensen 116br/1, Time & Life Pictures
26l, Time Life Pictures 26tr, UNICEF 51, Yellow Dog Productions 71;
Pearson Education Ltd: Gareth Boden 8, 9tl, 9tr, 9bl, 9br, 14, 24,
34, 48, 58, 68, 82, 92, 102, 112tl, 112br, 113bl, 114tl, 114tr, 115bl,
116tl, 116tr, 117l; **Photoshot Holdings Limited:** Jeff Blackler 79r;
Press Association Images: Clive Chilvers / Demotix 78cr, Ed Garvey
/ Manchester City FC 123bl; **PYMCA:** Mr Hartnett 53tl; **Reuters:**
Karoly Arvai 84r; **Rex Features:** 110, Albanpix Ltd 29tl, 29tr, 29b,
Albanpix Ltd 29tl, 29tr, 29b, c.Warner Br / Everett 52, Charles Bowman
/ Robert Harding 124tl, Geoffrey Robinson 99cl/a, The World of Sports
SC 26br, Universal / Everett 124br; **Jorge Rodriguez-Gerada:** 84l;
Shutterstock.com: 90, Lance Bellers 109, Brandon Blinkenberg
126cr, Louise Cukrov 19tl, Jaimie Duplass 56, Warren Goldswain 55bl,
gudak 99bl/b, Dmitriy Shironosov 76; **SuperStock:** Andrew Michael
/ age fotostock 121tr, Antoine Juliette / Oredia / Oredia Eurl 116br/3,
Image Source 65l, Mark Beton / age fotostock 61, OJO Images
116br/4, Prisma 19br, 20cr, Prisma 19br, 20cr, Robert Harding Picture
Library 121bl, The Irish Image Collection 122br, Tom Bol / Aurora
Open 55cr, Werner Otto / age fotostock 116br/5; **The Kobal
Collection:** Warner Bros 89; **TopFoto:** The Granger Collection 104br;
www.tumbleweedhouses.com: 11

All other images © Pearson Education Limited

Cover image: *Front:* **Shutterstock.com:** Corepics VOF

Every effort has been made to trace the copyright holders and we
apologise in advance for any unintentional omissions. We would be
pleased to insert the appropriate acknowledgement in any subsequent
edition of this publication.

Special thanks to the following for their help during location
photography:
Brighton & Hove City Council; Debden Park High School and students;
Hertford Library, East Area Libraries, Hertfordshire County Council;
Herts & Essex Hospital; By kind permission of the Natural History
Museum, London www.nhm.ac.uk; The Rosen family; www.cyberdog.
net; www.locationworks.com

Illustrated by: Andy Robert Davies pages 10, 13, 17, 64; Paula Franco
pages 4, 5, 22, 33, 44, 54, 57, 91, 114, 115; Peskimo pages 16, 30,
70, 94, 99; Zara Picken pages 6, 122, 126; Gary Rose pages 39, 74,
80, 112; Ben Steers pages 23, 90, 98, 101, 120.